NEW Grammar Time 3

Teacher's Book

Sandy Jervis and Maria Carling

PEARSON
Longman

Pearson Education Limited
Edinburgh Gate
Harlow
Essex CM20 2JE
England
and Associated Companies throughout the World.

www.longman.com

© Pearson Education Limited 2008

All rights reserved; no part of this publication may be reproduced, stored in a retrieval system, or transmitted in any form or by any means, electronic, mechanical, photocopying, recording, or otherwise without the prior written permission of the Publishers.

The right of Sandy Jervis and Maria Carling to be identified as author of this work has been asserted by her in accordance with the Copyright, Designs and Patents Act 1988.

First published 2001
This edition 2008

Teachers Book ISBN: 978-1-4058-5273-9

Printed in Malaysia , KHL CTP

Set in Ulissa 10pt

Cover by Mackerel Design.
Illustrations by Stephen May.
Designed and Project Managed by Starfish Design
Editorial and Project Management Ltd.

NEW Grammar Time 3

Teacher's Book

Contents

- Introduction — 4
- Answer key — 7
- Photocopiable activities — 26
- Photocopiable activity sheets — 35
- Photocopiable quiz sheets — 59
- Progress checks — 71

Introduction

Grammar Time is a series of grammar reference and practice books specifically designed for young learners from the age of eight upwards. **Grammar Time** can be used alongside any major coursebook. The aims and overall purpose of the series are:

- to present grammar in amusing, meaningful contexts, appropriate to the pupils' age and level.
- to help them understand new grammatical items by means of simple reference tables and explanations of key points.
- to help them assimilate the grammar by providing interesting, graded practice exercises.
- to provide opportunities to use the grammar communicatively in freer oral and/or written practice.

Grammar Time and the Common European Framework

The new editions of **Grammar Time** are closely correlated to the Common European Framework.

Grammar Time	Language level	Common European Framework	Cambridge ESOL
1	Beginners		Starters
2	False beginners	A1	Movers
3	Elementary	A2	Flyers, KET
4	Pre-Intermediate	B1	PET
5	Intermediate	B1+ (towards B2)	

Grammar Time components

The components of the course are:
- a Pupils' Book
- a Teacher's Resource Book with answer keys and additional photocopiable activities, unit quizzes and progress checks
- a Multi-Rom containing recorded material from the Pupils' Book that can be played on a CD player for use in the classroom; and extra practice exercises for the learners to do at home on their computers

Grammar Time syllabus progression

The order in which grammatical items are introduced in **Grammar Time** follows the typical progression of most coursebooks. However, it is possible to select units in any order which is relevant and appropriate to the particular needs of your language classroom.

Organisation of Grammar Time 3 Pupils' Book

The main part of the book consists of:
- twenty-five core units
- five revision units called 'Use your English'

Additional reference material at the end of the book consists of:
- quick check verb form tables
- spelling rules
- unit by unit wordlist

Grammar Time Characters

There are recurring characters in Grammar Time 3-5: Harry Banks, Beth MacKenzie, Peter and Lucy Hardy. They all go to the same school – Peter and Harry are in the same class, Beth and Lucy are in the class below them.

- Harry is 12 years old. He is the editor of 'TeenLink', the school magazine. He loves basketball and watching DVDs with his friends.
- Beth is 11 years old. She's an assistant editor on 'TeenLink' and is a keen reporter. She's very intelligent and has lots of good ideas for the magazine.
- Peter is Harry's best friend. He's 12 years old. He loves sport and enjoys teasing his little sister, Lucy.
- Lucy is 11 years old. She's artistic and very strong-minded.
- Cosmo and Bella are Harry's cats, although they spend a lot of time at Peter and Lucy's house.

Core units

Each core unit is organised in the following way.

Presentation

Motivating and memorable content facilitates the acquisition of language. In **Grammar Time 3**, grammar is presented in context through cartoons featuring the four main characters, the two cats and their friends. Pupils can easily identify with the varied and amusing situations the characters find themselves in. The cartoons are recorded on the accompanying Multi-Rom.

Care has been taken so that larger "chunks" of grammar are broken down to make them more manageable for young learners. In **Grammar Time 3**, units vary in length according to the language item introduced. In Unit 14, for instance, which deals with the past simple, the first three pages present and practise the regular form of the past simple only. The following three pages present and practise the irregular form and the final spread brings all the forms together, reinforcing the work done in the previous six pages. This gives you some freedom to adapt the

Introduction

pace according to the needs of each individual class, choosing either to break down the unit into two or even three different lessons, or to deal with the whole unit at one go.

Grammar reference tables and explanations

The grammar reference tables help focus the learners' attention on the new grammatical items in a visually memorable way. Students are often asked to complete the tables themselves, using language extracted from the presentation cartoons.

Following the tables is a Grammar Box, with explanations of form and use, which provides further clear examples of the grammar in context.

The tables and explanations appear together before the practice section. This makes it easy for pupils to refer to them while working through the exercises.

Exercises

The controlled practice exercises that follow each presentation are carefully graded to ensure that new language can be easily consolidated. They aim to recycle known vocabulary rather than introduce a large number of new lexical items, which would only serve to confuse and distract the pupils. The cartoon characters often appear in the exercises to provide realistic contexts for the grammatical items.

Each unit ends with a writing exercise, so that learners can put the new language they have learnt into use. Learners are given a clear model to follow and are then guided through the process of producing their own written work.

'Use your English' revision units

There are five revision units in the book. They allow for regular consolidation of the language presented and practised so far. The tasks aim to provide realistic and communicative contexts for the language to make it more memorable. Again, the lexis used is familiar to the learner.

Reference material

At the end of book, there are:
- an irregular verb list
- spelling rules for plural nouns, the third person singular (*he, she, it*), past simple, comparatives and superlatives, and verbs + *-ing*.

These provide a fast and simple way to review or revise these grammar areas.

Wordlist

This contains key lexical items from each unit. Your pupils may want to write in a translation of each word in their own language. They can use this for reference at home and for revision purposes.

For you, this list proves a preview of which words your pupils will need to know to be able to work alone on a unit. It can help you decide what key vocabulary to pre-teach before the Presentation.

Useful tips

Presentation

One of the main advantages of this series is its use of recurring cartoon characters which present grammar through amusing stories. The presentations are recorded on the Multi-ROM accompanying the Pupils' Book.

You can start off by asking pupils to look at the pictures and say what they think is happening. Depending on the linguistic level and perception of their class, you might find it useful to pre-teach key lexical items that appear in the presentation (using the wordlist if necessary).

You can then play the recording and either have the pupils follow in their books, or listen with books closed. It's a good idea to play the recording twice. The second time, you can ask pupils to repeat parts of the dialogue.

After listening to the recording, allow pupils to comment on the stories and give their opinions.

Follow-up ideas
- Pupils can act out the dialogues in class immediately.
- Pupils can be assigned to learn the lines of one of the characters for homework and act out the dialogues in the next lesson without books.
- You could write the dialogue on the board, leaving out key grammatical items, then ask pupils to fill them in.
- Pupils may be encouraged to write their own version of the story making any desirable changes (this can be done in class with the teacher as a resource; pupils then vote for the best version).

Grammar reference tables and explanations

It is advisable for you to go through these in class, before pupils work on the exercises. Pupils can be asked to read the items in the tables aloud (in chorus and individually) to familiarise themselves with pronunciation and stress. You can ask them to supply further examples based on the tables.

Draw your pupils' attention to any additional explanations, and make certain that they understand, adding extra examples on the board if you wish.

When this is done, pupils could be asked to go back to the presentation and circle, underline or highlight all grammatical items in focus.

Controlled practice exercises

The simple instructions and examples provided make all exercises suitable for homework. However, it is always advisable to do a sufficient number of them in class, where you can prompt, help and advise. If necessary, do more than one item as an example and ask pupils to work through the rest of the activity individually or, preferably, in pairs.

Pupils should be encouraged to ask questions if they are in difficulty. You can usually guide them towards finding the answer on their own by looking back at the presentation and tables.

When it is time for checking, it is a good idea to encourage the rest of the class to say whether a particular answer given is acceptable or not, rather than accepting or correcting immediately. Multiple choice exercises or those which require a choice between two words (e.g. *was* or *were*), make them suitable for "voting" – that is, pupils are asked to put their hands up to choose one of the answers (the majority is usually right).

'Use your English' revision units

The 'Use your English' revision units are best done in class, as they contain speaking exercises as well as written exercises.

Teacher's Resource Book

This Teacher's Resource Book contains answer keys to all the exercises in the Pupils' Book, as well as additional photocopiable activities with teaching notes, Unit Quizzes and Progress Checks with answer keys.

Photocopiable activities

There is one photocopiable activity sheet for each unit in the Pupils' Book (apart from Units 20-21 which are both covered in one activity sheet). The activities consist of games and pairwork activities to activate the language practised in the unit in a lively and interesting way. This provides another opportunity to recycle the grammar and build your pupils' confidence in using the language.

The teaching notes explain how to use each activity and answers are provided where necessary.

Unit Quizzes and Progress Checks

There is a photocopiable Quiz for every two units in the Pupils' Book. The style of the tasks is appropriate for the assessment of language use at this level.

The Quizzes are best done in class after the completion of a unit and after homework has been checked. They do not take long and are a valuable form of assessment.

In addition, there are five Progress Checks, which review the same units as the 'Use your English' revision units. They help you assess which grammatical areas you may need to return to. They also highlight individual weaknesses for future revision.

It might be best for you to collect the Quizzes and Progress Checks and correct them before returning them to the pupils with the score and your comments. Comments should be positive and encouraging wherever possible.

With some classes, it helps to create an atmosphere of competition. You can do this by announcing at the beginning of the book that the three pupils with the highest overall score at the end of the year will receive a special commendation certificate or prize.

Multi-ROM / CD-ROM

The Multi-ROM or CD-ROM packaged with each Pupils' Book contains

For the teacher:
- 60 minutes of recorded material from the Pupils' Book, including all the Presentation cartoons and the final Speaking exercises. Some of the other cartoons and dialogues are also recorded, to allow pupils to listen and check their answers. This material can be played on an ordinary CD player. A 🎧 symbol indicates when an exercise is recorded.

For the pupils:
- extra practice exercises and games which can be done on a home computer. For each unit, there are up to five extra exercises including at least one listening exercise, as well as a final game to make learning fun. There are also five revision units for further consolidation. Only vocabulary that has been seen in the Pupils' Book is used, to facilitate pupils' understanding and allow them to focus on the grammar.

Key to the Pupils' Book

Unit 1

1

I	am ('m)
You/We/They	are ('re)
He/She/It	is ('s)
I	am not
You/We/They	are not (aren't)
He/She/It	is not (isn't)
Am I?	Yes, I am. / No, I'm not.
Are you?/we?/they?	Yes, you/we/they are. / No, he/she/it isn't.

What/Who am I?
Where/Who are you?/we?/they?
Where/Who is he?/she?/it?

3
1. are
2. is
3. is
4. are
5. is
6. am
7. are
8. are

4
1. I
2. 's
3. 're
4. 'm
5. It
6. 's
7. He
8. 's
9. She
10. They
11. 's
12. We

5
1. Beth isn't eight. She's
2. Harry isn't at school. He's
3. Peter and Harry aren't cousins. They're
4. London isn't in China. It's
5. Giraffes aren't short. They're
6. Italy isn't a big city. It's
7. I'm not Tim's sister. I'm
8. Anna isn't from Turkey. She's

6
1. Is Peter Lucy's cousin? No, he isn't.
2. Are Cosmo and Bella dogs? No, they aren't.
3. Is Beth a doctor? No, she isn't.
4. Are Peter and Harry neighbours? Yes, they are.
5. Is Lucy Harry's sister? No, she isn't.
6. Is Harry Peter's friend? Yes, he is.
7. Are Peter and Lucy twins? No, they aren't.
8. Is *TeenLink* the new school magazine? Yes, it is.

7
1. Ben
2. Twelve
3. London
4. Class 8c
5. Geography
6. 1.5 metres

8
1. How old are you? I'm …
2. When's your birthday? It's on …
3. Are you a student? Yes, I am.
4. Where's your school. It's …
5. Is your classroom big? Yes, it is. / No, it isn't.
6. What is your teacher's name? It's …
7. What's in your bag?
8. Is English your favourite subject? Yes, it is. / No, it isn't.

9
1. I'm twelve
2. I'm the editor
3. I'm in class 6C
4. My classroom isn't very big
5. we're neighbours
6. Is your classroom big

10
(Students' own answers)

Unit 2

1

This is an umbrella.   These are sweets.
That's a rucksack.   Those are biscuits.

This is an apple. The apple is for Lucy
These are biscuits. The biscuits are for me.

3
1. these
2. those
3. this
4. that
5. those
6. this
7. these
8. that
9. those
10. these
11. this
12. that

4
1. These
2. This
3. This
4. this
5. This
6. That
7. these
8. This
9. These
10. Those
11. these
12. These
13. Those
14. these
15. those

5
1. Is this; it isn't
2. Are these; they aren't
3. Is that; it is
4. Are those, they are
5. Are these, they aren't
6. Is that, it is

6
1. The, the
2. an, –; The, the
3. –, –; The, the
4. an, a; The, the
5. a, – ; The, the

7
1. –
2. a
3. The
4. the
5. a
6. a
7. a
8. –

8
apples
beaches
ladies
knives

9

-s	-es
boys	classes
computers	dresses
days	foxes
faces	tomatoes
pens	

-ies	-ves
babies	knives
cities	leaves
families	shelves
lorries	wives
wolves	strawberries

Irregular
feet
mice
people
sheep
watches
women

Grammar Time 3

10
1. These photos are fantastic!
2. Those bags are heavy.
3. These stories are very funny!
4. Those women are from London.
5. These dresses are beautiful.
6. Those boys are very tall.
7. These radios are expensive.
8. These knives are sharp.

11
1. Koalas
2. noses
3. eyes
4. feet
5. tails
6. leaves
7. kilos
8. people
9. Tigers
10. cats
11. legs
12. teeth
13. leaves
14. deer
15. monkeys
16. fish

12
1. b
2. c
3. b
4. c
5. b
6. a
7. c
8. c

13
1. This
2. The
3. a
4. a
5. a
6. these
7. glasses
8. shelves
9. the
10. an
11. posters

14
(Students' own answers)

Unit 3

1
That's Beth's salad.
Are those the boys' bikes?
Look at those women's clothes!
Look at the colour of that car!

3
1. Harry's
2. Helen's
3. sister's
4. Lucy's
5. Cosmo's
6. David's
7. boy's
8. Bella's

4
1. Chris's / Chris'
2. Anne's, James's / James'
3. girls'
4. cousin's
5. Stella's
6. Giles's / Giles'
7. Jade's
8. sisters'

5
1. Robert and Sophie's
2. children's
3. aunt's
4. parents'
5. Marie and Tess's
6. women's
7. Cosmo and Bella's
8. girls'

6
1. grandparents'
2. friends'
3. children's
4. men's
5. Phil and David's
6. Charles'
7. women's
8. parents'

7
1. Bella is Harry's cat.
2. That is Helen's mum.
3. Emma's bag is on the chair.
4. It is Jo's birthday today.
5. Mike is Sarah's cousin.
6. Sam's computer is fantastic.
7. Eric's father is a doctor.
8. My dog's name is Bono.

8
1. it's Tony's
2. they're Mrs Cooper's
3. it's Kevin's
4. they're Mr Jones'
5. it's Ruth and Becky's
6. they're Diane's
7. it's James'
8. they're my brothers'

9
1. the top of the page
2. the roof of that house
3. end of the road
4. colour of your dress
5. capital of France
6. end of this story
7. top of the mountain
8. back of our house

10
1. name of your street
2. your teacher's name
3. walls of your room
4. your dad's hair
5. capital of France
6. your sister's favourite music
7. the cat's food
8. your friend's brother

11
1. dad's boat
2. name of the boat
3. Sophie's brother
4. Ben's favourite sport
5. dog's name
6. Ben and Sophie's dog
7. James' hobby
8. Sandra's mum

12
(Students' own answers)

Unit 4

1

I/You/We/They	have got ('ve got)
He/She/It	has got ('s got)
I/You/We/They	have not got (haven't got)
He/She/It	has not got (hasn't got)
Have I/we/you/they got a bike?	Yes, I/you/we/they have. / No, I/you/we/they haven't.
Has he/she/it got a bike?	Yes, he/she/it has. / No, he/she/it hasn't.

3
1. have got
2. has got
3. have got
4. have got
5. have got
6. has got

4
1. She is my best friend.
2. She has got blue eyes.
3. Dave is Susan's brother.
4. Dave has got a new computer.
5. Becky's sister has got short hair.
6. Becky is twelve years old.
7. He is at home.
8. He has got a headache.

5
1. Samantha's got a laptop.
2. Lee and Kim have got an MP3 player.
3. Samantha hasn't got a mobile phone.
4. Lee and Kim haven't got a camera.
5. Samantha hasn't got an MP3 player.
6. Lee and Kim have got a laptop.
7. I have / haven't got a laptop.
8. I have / haven't got a camera.

Answer key

6
1 Yes, I have. / No, I haven't.
2 Yes, I have. / No, I haven't.
3 Yes, I have. / No, I haven't.
4 Yes, it has. / No, it hasn't.
5 Yes s/he has. / No, s/he hasn't.
6 Yes, it has. / No, it hasn't.
7 Yes, they have. / No, they haven't.
8 Yes, they have. / No, they haven't.

7
1 Has Beth got black hair? No, she hasn't. She's got brown hair.
2 Has Harry got blond hair? Yes, he has.
3 Has Lucy got brown hair? No, she hasn't. She's got red hair.
4 Has Beth got a big nose? No, she hasn't. She's got a small nose.
5 Has Peter got a sister? Yes, he has.
6 Has Harry got two cats? Yes, he has.
7 Has Peter got blue jeans? No, he hasn't. He's got purple trousers.
8 Has Lucy got a green shirt? Yes, she has.

8
1 've   4 got
2 have   5 Have
3 've   6 got

9
me	my	mine
you	your	yours
he	his	his
she	her	hers
it	its	its
we	our	ours
you	your	yours
they	their	theirs

Whose bag is this? It's hers.
Whose shoes are these? They're mine.

11
1 Our
2 Its
3 His
4 Their
5 their
6 Our
7 His
8 Her
9 your
10 My

12
1 It's mine.
2 It's not ours.
3 It's yours.
4 They're his.
5 It's not theirs.
6 They're yours.
7 It's hers.
8 They're not mine.

13
1 Whose, are
2 Whose, is; hers
3 Whose, is; theirs
4 Whose, are; yours
5 Whose, are; his
6 Whose, is; mine
7 Whose, are; ours
8 Whose, is; hers

14
1 your
2 yours, hers
3 ours
4 her
5 our, my
6 yours
7 Their
8 theirs
9 hers
10 my

15
1 My
2 Our
3 He's
4 He's got
5 his
6 have
7 My
8 hers

16
(Students' own answers)

Unit 5

1
There are not (aren't)
Are there?
Yes, there are.
No, there isn't.

3
1 There's, Lucy's
  There's, Beth's
2 There are, Beth's
  There are Lucy's
3 There is, Beth's
  There is, Lucy's
4 There are, Lucy's
  There are, Beth's
5 There is, Beth's
  There is, Lucy's

4
1 Is there; No, there isn't.
2 Are there; Yes, there are.
3 Are there; No, there aren't.
4 Are there; Yes, there are.
5 Is there; Yes, there is.
6 Is there; No, there isn't.
7 Is there; No, there isn't.
8 Are there; Yes, there are.

5
1 Where's Peter's; It's under
2 Where are; They're on
3 Where is; It's behind
4 Where is; It's between
5 Where are; They're next to
6 Where are; They're opposite

6 (11)
1 at   6 on
2 at   7 at
3 in   8 at
4 to   9 at
5 on

7
1 near   5 There's
2 in   6 opposite
3 near   7 next
4 there are

8
(Students' own answers)

Use your English 1

1 (12)
Audioscript
1 Where's Sarah's bag?
A: There's your bag, Sarah. It's on that chair.
B: No, that isn't my bag. It's Carol's.
A: Where's your bag, then?
B: It's here – under the chair.

2 Where's the supermarket?
B: Excuse me …
A: Yes?
B: Is there a supermarket near here?
A: Yes, it's over there, on the right. Oh no, wait – The post office is on the right. The supermarket's on the left. Sorry!
B: Thank you.

3 Which photo is from the birthday party?
B: Look. Here's a photo from my birthday party.
A: Let me see. Oh – is this Emma?
B: Yes. And Kate's next to her.
A: Where?
B: Here – next to Emma. Look.

4 Where's the cinema?
B: There's a new cinema in West Street.
A: Really? Where?
B: It's between the flower shop and the café. It's great!
A: Let's go there tonight, then!

5 Where's the umbrella?
A: What's the matter?
B: I can't find my umbrella! It isn't in my bag and it isn't on my bed…
A: It's behind that door.
B: Where?

Grammar Time 3

A: Over there, Jess! Behind the door!
B: Oh, thanks!

1 c   4 c
2 a   5 c
3 b

2
1 that
2 hasn't got
3 Whose
4 mine
5 these
6 her
7 haven't got
8 Is
9 there
10 a

3
1 B   6 C
2 A   7 B
3 C   8 C
4 A   9 B
5 B   10 B

4
1 I'm … years old.
2 I'm from …
3 Yes, I have. I've got … sister and … brother. / No, I haven't.
4 My favourite subject is …
5 My best friend's name's …

Unit 6

1
Do not (Don't) leave me alone.
Do not (Don't) pull.

I you he she it we you they
me you him her it us you them

3
1 Tidy   4 Listen
2 Help   5 Open
3 Come   6 Look

4
1 Don't open
2 Don't wear
3 Don't sit
4 Don't buy
5 Don't play
6 Don't call

5
1 Do not walk
2 Wash
3 do not feed
4 Do not take
5 Drive
6 Call

6
1 Let's
2 don't
3 Let's
4 Don't
5 Don't
6 Let's
7 Let's
8 Don't

7
1 I   5 me
2 We   6 She's
3 they   7 them
4 us   8 her

8
1 them   4 us
2 him   5 them
3 you   6 me

9
1 Look
2 Don't touch
3 us
4 it
5 Don't be
6 Let's
7 go
8 take
9 her

10
1 f   4 e
2 c   5 a
3 b   6 d

11
(suggested answer)
Take an apple, a carrot and an orange.
Peel the fruit and then slice it.
Put the fruit into a blender.
Push the button.
Pour the fruit juice into a glass.

Unit 7

1
I/You/We/They do not (don't) play

Do I/we/you/they play?
No, I/you/we/they don't.

Does he/she/it play?
Yes, he/she/it does.

3
-s	-es	-ies
answers	fixes	carries
closes	goes	cries
likes	teaches	flies
starts	washes	tidies
stays	watches	worries

4
1 watches
2 likes
3 closes
4 visit
5 eat
6 lives
7 tidy
8 start
9 teaches
10 fly

5 (16)
1 gets up
2 drinks
3 has
4 plays
5 watches
6 eats
7 goes out
8 stays

6
1 doesn't play; plays
2 don't live; live
3 doesn't write; writes
4 don't have; have
5 don't eat; eat
6 don't drink; drink
7 don't like; like
8 don't study; study

7
1 Does, live; Yes, he does.
2 Do, get up; No, they don't.
3 Does, drink; Yes, he does.
4 Does, play; No, she doesn't.
5 Do, drink; Yes, they do.
6 Does, get up; No, he doesn't.
7 Do, play; Yes, they do.
8 Does, live; Yes, she does.

8
1 Do you walk to school every day? Yes, I do. / No, I don't.
2 Do your lessons start at eight o'clock? Yes, they do. / No, they don't.
3 Do you do your homework every night? Yes, I do. / No, I don't.
4 Do you and your best friend got to the same school? Yes, we do. / No, we don't.
5 Do you watch TV after school? Yes, I do. / No, I don't.
6 Does your best friend visit you at weekends? Yes, s/he does. / No, s/he doesn't.
7 Do you play sport every day? Yes, I do. / No, I don't.
8 Does your mum get up early at weekends? Yes, she does. / No, she doesn't.

Answer key

9
1. Do you go
2. do they live
3. do you go
4. does Sam play
5. do you do
6. does Zoe go
7. do you want
8. does your sister work

10
1. b
2. d
3. f
4. c
5. h
6. g
7. a
8. e

11
1. at
2. on
3. at, on
4. twice
5. in
6. every
7. every
8. in
9. on

12
1. What time do you get up in the morning?
2. When do you do your homework?
3. What do you do in your free time?
4. How often do you go to the sports centre?
5. Do you play computer games?
6. Do you listen to classical music?
7. What time do you go to bed?
8. When does your family go on holiday?

13
1. get up
2. don't go
3. don't have
4. comes
5. listen
6. takes
7. go
8. have
9. Does your school close
10. do you spend

14 & 15
(Students' own answers)

Unit 8

1
I usually have cornflakes.
My mum often makes pancakes.
I sometimes have milk.
I never eat fruit.

5
1. doesn't always have
2. don't usually eat
3. 'm never
4. doesn't always go
5. don't often wear
6. isn't always
7. doesn't usually rain
8. doesn't often get up

6
1. Does Harry often walk to school? Yes, he does.
2. Does Peter always eat fruit? No, he doesn't. He sometimes eats fruit.
3. Is Beth usually late for school? No, she isn't. She's never late for school
4. Does Lucy often go to the zoo? Yes, she does.
5. Does Cosmo always eat a lot? Yes, he does.
6. Does Izumi sometimes get up late? No, she doesn't. She never gets up late.

7
1. I never eat burgers
2. My brother eats burgers once a week.
3. My dad plays golf every weekend.
4. My mum sometimes plays tennis.
5. What time do you usually have lunch?
6. What time do you have supper on Saturdays.
7. Do you often go to the sports centre?
8. Does your brother go to the sports centre twice a week?

8
1. do you usually do
2. always visit
3. Do you visit them
4. do you go
5. never go
6. goes there once a week
7. do you do on Sundays
8. usually stay
9. watch my favourite programme in the morning
10. do my homework in the afternoon

9
1. always
2. on
3. never
4. at
5. in
6. sometimes
7. In
8. never

10
(Students' own answers)

Unit 9

1
I am ('m) painting
We/You/They are ('re) painting
He/She/It is ('s) painting

I am not ('m not) painting
We/You/They are not (aren't) painting
He/She/It is not (isn't) painting
Am I painting?
Yes, I am. / No, I'm not.
Are we/you/they painting?
Yes, you/we/they are. / No, you/we/they aren't.
Is he/she/it painting?
Yes, he/she/it is. / No, he/she/it isn't.

3

-ing	e + -ing	double consonant + -ing
asking	closing	beginning
buying	dancing	running
opening	driving	sitting
talking	leaving	stopping
watching	smiling	swimming

4
1. 're having
2. 's cooking
3. 's making
4. 's taking
5. are playing
6. 's writing
7. are sitting
8. 's sleeping
9. 're having
10. 'm wearing

5
1. Sonia isn't opening the door. She's opening the window.
2. Maya isn't washing her face. She's washing her brushes.
3. Liam and Dan aren't painting. They're eating.
4. Lucy isn't talking to Sonia. She's talking to the teacher.
5. Tom and Alan aren't carrying a chair. They're carrying a parcel/box.
6. Keisha isn't writing in her notebook. She's painting.
7. Sue isn't standing on a box. She's standing on a chair/stool.

6
1. Is Sonia painting? No, she isn't.
2. Are Tom and Alan talking to the teacher? No, they aren't.
3. Is Nick drinking water? Yes, he is.
4. Is Maya washing her brushes? Yes, she is.
5. Is Keisha opening the window? No, she isn't.
6. Are Liam and Dan eating? Yes, they are.
7. Is Sue standing on a chair? Yes, she is.

7
1. 're playing
2. are you doing
3. 'm watching
4. 's making
5. 's reading
6. isn't working

Grammar Time 3

7 he playing
8 isn't
9 's listening
10 's dancing

8
He isn't playing football at the moment.
We're not staying at home today.
She always has breakfast at eight o'clock.

10
1 does; 's going
2 writes; 's studying
3 tidy; 're visiting
4 plays; 's watching

11
1 are watching
2 aren't going
3 isn't sleeping
4 visit
5 Is Lucy playing
6 's wearing
7 Does Emma tidy
8 Is your father working
9 brush
10 Does your mother clean

12
1 Do; Yes, I do. / No, I don't.
2 Is; Yes, she is. / No, she isn't.
3 Do; Yes, they do. / No, they don't.
4 Is; Yes, it is. / No, it isn't.
5 Does; Yes s/he does. / No, s/he doesn't.
6 Does; Yes, s/he does. / No, s/he doesn't.
7 Are; Yes, I am. / No, I'm not.
8 Do; Yes, I do. / No, I don't.

13
1 go
2 have
3 spend
4 're having
5 're helping
6 's washing
7 'm making
8 'm not making
9 'm writing
10 are you doing

14
(Students' own answers)

Unit 10

1
Cycling is my favourite sport
He/She/It likes/loves/hates painting.

He/She/It is fond of singing
reading magazines.

I'd love to visit London.
I want to be a doctor.

3
1 Skating
2 Swimming
3 Fishing
4 Walking
5 Playing
6 Skiing
7 Surfing
8 jumping

4
1 Diane hates playing chess.
2 Steve likes listening to music.
3 Diane likes doing sport.
4 Steve hates dancing.
5 Diane loves listening to music.
6 Steve loves doing sport.

5
1 Do you like doing sport? Yes, I do. / No, I don't.
2 Do you enjoy learning English? Yes, I do. / No, I don't.
3 Do your friends like cycling? Yes, they do. / No, they don't.
4 Do you hate visiting museums? Yes, I do. / No, I don't.
5 Do your friends enjoy writing emails? Yes, they do. / No, they don't.
6 Does your mum like shopping? Yes, she does. / No, she doesn't.
7 Does your dad like swimming? Yes, he does. / No, he doesn't.
8 Do you enjoy going to the park? Yes, I do. / No, I don't.

6
1 on   5 about
2 at   6 of
3 in   7 on
4 at   8 with

7
1 to buy   5 to visit
2 to go   6 to have
3 to be   7 to do
4 to work   8 to stay

8
1 shopping 5 to live
2 to be   6 going
3 taking   7 to come
4 painting 8 to wear

9
1 c   5 b
2 b   6 a
3 b   7 b
4 a   8 c

10
(Students' own answers)

Use your English 2

1
🎧 21
Audioscript
1 When does David go to the swimming pool?
A: Do you do any sports, David?
B: Yes, I do. I play volleyball with my friends on Wednesdays.
A: That's good.
B: I also go swimming with my dad. We usually go to the sports centre swimming pool at the weekend because he works late during the week. Oh, I have a karate class on Mondays, as well.

2 What is the girl bad at doing?
A: I love playing computer games. Do you?
B: I like computer games, yeah.
A: I'm very good at skating, too.
B: Oh, no! I'm really bad at it. I always fall down. I'm good at riding a bike, though. I'm very fast.

3 What does the man do every day at six o'clock?
A: Can you pick up the boys from their French class tonight?
B: What time?
A: Their lesson finishes at a quarter to six.
B: But I always walk the dog at half past five and then I watch the news on TV at six o'clock!
A: Well, walk the dog at half past eight and watch the nine o'clock news, today!

4 What is Katy doing?
A: Sorry I'm late! Where is everybody?
B: Nadia is making the sandwiches and Tom is at the supermarket.
A: What about Katy?
B: She's choosing CDs for the party. No, wait! She's helping Tom with the shopping. The CDs are ready.

5 What does the boy do on Saturdays?
A: I'm bored!
B: Let's go to the cinema.
A: I don't like the films this week.
B: Go out with your friends, then. You always go out with them on Saturdays.
A: They want to go to the cinema!
B: OK. Help me with the garden, then. Come on! Get up! Hey, where are you going?
A: To the cinema with my friends!

1 b   4 a
2 c   5 b
3 a

2
1 D 4 F
2 G 5 A
3 B 6 H

3
1 with her Granny
2 a small garden
3 go for a walk
4 a special cake
5 Ginger
6 give Ginger food

4
(Students' own answers)

Unit 11

1
There are some bananas in the bowl
There is some yoghurt in the fridge.
There aren't any bananas in the bowl.
Are there any bananas in the bowl?
Is there any yoghurt in the fridge?

3
Countable nouns **Uncountable nouns**

Singular	Plural	
biscuit	apples	yoghurt
can	bottles	bread
egg	children	cheese
knife	feet	coffee
poster	mice	meat
table	sandwiches	tea

4
23
1 a   5 a
2 some 6 some
3 a   7 a
4 some 8 some

5
1 are some
2 isn't any
3 are some / are four
4 aren't any
5 is some
6 isn't any
7 are some
8 aren't any

6
1 Are there any biscuits? Yes, there are.
2 Is there any popcorn? Yes, there is.
3 Are there any bananas? No, there aren't.
4 Is there any milk? No, there isn't.
5 Are there any sandwiches? No, there aren't.
6 Is there any yoghurt? No, there isn't.
7 Are there any burgers? Yes, there are.
8 Is there any water? Yes, there is.

7
1 any 5 any
2 no   6 no
3 no   7 any
4 any 8 no

8
They're going somewhere.
There isn't anything in this box.
Is there anybody there?
Are they going anywhere?
They're going nowhere.

10
1 someone
2 anywhere
3 nothing
4 something
5 anything
6 no-one

11
1 Someone's
2 something
3 anyone
4 nothing
5 anywhere
6 no-one
7 anything
8 somewhere

12
1 No, there isn't any fruit in my schoolbag. / Yes, there are two apples in my schoolbag.
2 No, there aren't any sweets in my kitchen at home. / Yes, there are some sweets in my kitchen at home.
3 No, there isn't anything on my desk. / Yes, there is/are … on my desk.
4 No, I haven't got anything in my pocket. / Yes, there is/are … in my pocket.
5 No, there isn't anyone in my house at the moment. / Yes, there is/are … in my house at the moment.
6 No, no-one in my family speaks Chinese. / Yes, my … speaks Chinese.

13
25
1 nothing
2 something
3 any
4 some
5 any
6 some
7 nothing
8 someone
9 some

Unit 12

1
We've got a lot of cola.
We haven't got a lot of hot dogs.
How many hot dogs have we got?
How much cola have we got?

3
1 a carton of milk - e
2 a tin of soup - g
3 a slice of pizza - b
4 a bottle of water - d
5 a kilo of flour - h
6 a bar of chocolate - c
7 a loaf of bread - f
8 a can of cola – a

4
1 two cartons
2 three bottles
3 one packet
4 five cans
5 two kilos
6 four tins
7 three bars
8 two loaves

5
1 a lot of
2 a lot of
3 much
4 many
5 a lot of
6 much
7 a lot of
8 many
9 a lot of
10 a lot of

6
1 How many; A lot
2 How much; Not much
3 How many; Three
4 How much / A lot
5 How many / Not many
6 How many / Six
7 How much / A litre
8 How much / Not much
9 How many / Eight
10 How many / A lot

7
27
1 much
2 much
3 lot
4 many
5 many
6 a
7 of
8 many
9 litres

Grammar Time 3

8
1. pieces
2. some
3. much
4. some / a lot of
5. any
6. piece
7. some / a bottle of
8. a can

9
(Students' own answers)

Unit 13

1

I/He/She/It was not (wasn't) at home.
You/We/They were not (weren't) asleep.

Was I/he/she/it at home?
Yes, I/he/she/it was.
Were you/we/they asleep?
No, you/we/they weren't.

When were you/we/they late?

3
1. was
2. was
3. was
4. were
5. were
6. was
7. was
8. were

4
1. He wasn't at school. He was at the sports centre.
2. She wasn't at the cinema. She was at home.
3. He wasn't at the shops. He was at the library.
4. She wasn't at school. She was at the dentist's.
5. They weren't at the park. They were in the garden.
6. They weren't at the cinema. They were at the theatre.
7. She wasn't at the theatre. She was at the hairdresser's.

5
1. Were you at home yesterday afternoon? No, I wasn't.
2. Were you at the cinema? Yes, I was.
3. Were Mick and Carol with you? No, they weren't.
4. Were they at the sports centre? Yes, they were.
5. Was the film good? No, it wasn't.
6. Was it a comedy? Yes, it was.
7. Was your brother at home? No, he wasn't.
8. Was he at the sports centre, too? Yes, he was.

6
1. Where were you yesterday morning?
2. How old were you two years ago?
3. Where were your parents last night?
4. When were you and your family on holiday last year?
5. Why were you sad last week?
6. What time was your best friend at school this morning?

7
1. There weren't
2. There were
3. There wasn't
4. there wasn't
5. There was
6. there was
7. there weren't

8
1. c
2. b
3. b
4. b
5. a
6. a
7. a
8. b
9. b

9
1. was
2. weren't
3. were
4. was
5. were
6. weren't
7. were
8. were
9. weren't
10. were

10
(Students' own answers)

Unit 14

1
I/You/He/She/It/We/They talked.
I/You/He/She/It/We/They did not (didn't) travel.
Did I/you/he/she/it/we/they talk?
No, I/you/he/she/it/we/they didn't.

3
1. played
2. weighed
3. collected
4. climbed
5. danced
6. scored

4
1. He didn't watch a film. He watched
2. They didn't play football. They played
3. I didn't study for my Maths test. I studied for my
4. She didn't bake a chocolate cake. She baked
5. She didn't phone Izumi. She phoned

5
1. Peter didn't tidy his room.
2. Sophie helped her teacher.
3. Harry finished his puzzle.
4. Lucy didn't play the violin.
5. Beth cooked spaghetti.
6. Mr Hardy didn't go to work.

6
1. Did Peter tidy the living room yesterday? No, he didn't.
2. Did Harry finish his puzzle? Yes, he did.
3. Did Beth cook fish? No, she didn't.
4. Did Lucy play the violin? No, she didn't.
5. Did Sophie help her teacher? Yes, she did.
6. Did Mr Hardy stay in bed? Yes, he did.

7
1. Did you enjoy
2. did
3. Did you stay
4. didn't
5. Did you talk
6. didn't
7. Did you visit
8. did

8
I/You/He/She/It/We/They did not (didn't) write.
Did I/you/he/she/it/we/they eat?
No, I/you/he/she/it/we/they didn't.

10
1. f
2. i
3. a
4. l
5. b
6. j
7. c
8. e
9. k
10. g
11. d
12. h

11
1. saw
2. got
3. wrote
4. did
5. made
6. ate
7. bought
8. read

12
1. He got up at 8.00.
2. He did his homework for Monday.
3. He told Mum about the concert.
4. He didn't get tickets for the concert.
5. He didn't buy any cat food for Cosmo and Bella.
6. He didn't send an email to David.
7. He met Harry at 5.30.

Answer key

13
1. Did Peter get up; Yes, he did.
2. Did he do; Yes, he did.
3. Did he tell; Yes, he did.
4. Did he get; No, he didn't.
5. Did he buy; No, he didn't.
6. Did he send; No, he didn't.
7. Did he meet; Yes, he did.

14
1. went
2. forgot
3. didn't go
4. didn't win
5. broke
6. lost
7. came
8. found
9. didn't have
10. waited
11. came

15
1. She went to the leisure centre.
2. No, she didn't.
3. Because she forgot her swimsuit.
4. No, it didn't.
5. She broke them.
6. Because Mum didn't have her keys.
7. He came back from work after two hours.

16
1. went
2. travelled
3. stayed
4. got up
5. swam
6. met
7. sent
8. visited

17
1. did you do
2. Did you stay
3. didn't
4. visited
5. Did you have
6. was
7. did you go
8. went
9. saw
10. Did you speak
11. did
12. got

18
1. What time did you get up last Saturday? I got up at …
2. Did you go shopping with a friend? Yes, I did. / No, I didn't.
3. What did you do in the afternoon?
4. Did a friend call you? Yes, s/he did. / No, s/he didn't.
5. Where did you go on Sunday? I went to …
6. Did you stay at home? Yes, I did. / No, I didn't.
7. Did you do any homework? Yes, I did. / No, I didn't.
8. What time did you do to bed? I went to bed at …

19
1. met
2. asked
3. talked
4. flew
5. wanted
6. Did you know
7. visited
8. played
9. left
10. take

20
(Students' own answers)

Use your English 3

1

Audioscript

🎧 31

1. What did the boy do on Saturday?
A: Did you go to the beach on Saturday?
B: No. My sister did, but I didn't go with her. I don't like swimming very much. I went to the sports centre with Mike.
A: Did you play tennis?
B: Well, yes. I wanted to play volleyball, but Mike didn't. He hates it!

2. Where was Fred this morning?
A: Where's Fred?
B: He's at the library with Dave. They're working on their Science project.
A: I called him this morning. Where was he?
B: He was the park.
A: Was Dave with him, too?
B: No, he wasn't. He was at home.

3. Where did the girls meet?
A: Did your mother drive you to the cinema last night?
B: No. She was busy.
A: Did you walk there?
B: No – we got the bus. I met Judy outside the bank at 7.30 and we walked to the bus stop. But our bus was late and we missed the beginning of the film.

4. How much milk do they need?
A: Do we need any flour for the cake?
B: Yes. And we need two eggs, a packet of sugar, a glass of water and a carton of milk.
A: Well, we've got everything we need, then. Let's make the cake!

5. What did Becky give Ben for his birthday?
A: So, did Ben like your present, Becky?
B: Yes, he did. He loved it.
A: You gave him a book, right?
B: No – I gave him a CD. I got it from that new music shop in Victoria Street.

1. c
2. b
3. a
4. b
5. a

2
1. How many
2. any
3. any
4. any
5. How much
6. How many
7. A lot!
8. anything

3
1. much
2. many
3. was
4. nothing
5. There
6. any
7. were
8. some
9. of

4
1. Were you busy last weekend?
2. Did you go to the cinema?
3. Did you visit a friend?
4. Did you watch TV?
5. Did you listen to music?
6. Did you do any homework?
7. How much money did you spend?
8. How many films did you watch?

5
1. had
2. took
3. went
4. wasn't
5. liked
6. didn't go
7. stayed
8. wanted
9. came
10. watched
11. Did you have
12. did you do

Unit 15

1
There was a good programme on TV.
That's a good idea!
I want to be an explorer.
I want to sail round the world.
Where's the Sahara Desert?
Let's explore the park!

3
1. a
2. an
3. an
4. an
5. the
6. the
7. a

Grammar Time 3

4
1 –, the
2 –, –
3 The, –
4 The, –
5 The, –
6 –, –
7 –, –
8 The, the
9 –, –
10 –, the

5
1 a
2 –
3 –
4 –
5 –
6 –
7 the
8 –
9 the
10 –
11 a

6
1 a, the
2 a, The
3 a, The, The
4 a, a, The, a
5 an, The
6 an, The

7
(Students' own answers)

8
1 –
2 the
3 a
4 The
5 a
6 a
7 –
8 The
9 the
10 –
11 the
12 –
13 the
14 the
15 a

9
(Students' own answers)

Unit 16

1
bigger than — the biggest
heavier than — the heaviest
lazier than — the laziest

3
strong	stronger	the strongest
thin	thinner	the thinnest
ugly	uglier	the ugliest
small	smaller	the smallest
big	bigger	the biggest
fast	faster	the fastest
pretty	prettier	the prettiest
nice	nicer	the nicest
fat	fatter	the fattest

4
1 smaller than
2 heavier than
3 longer than
4 higher than
5 bigger than
6 stronger than
7 cheaper than
8 larger than

5
1 The smallest
2 The largest
3 the loudest
4 The fatest
5 the slowest
6 The biggest
7 the noisiest
8 The longest

6
1 Peter's older than Lucy.
2 Peter's shorter than Harry.
3 Harry's heavier than Peter.
4 Beth's younger than Harry.
5 Lucy's thinner than Beth.
6 Beth's taller than Lucy.
7 Peter and Harry are the oldest.
8 Lucy's the shortest.
9 Harry's the heaviest.
10 Lucy's the youngest.
11 Lucy's the thinnest.
12 Harry's the tallest.

7
1 the tallest; – is the tallest.
2 younger than; Yes, I am.
3 easier than; No, it isn't.
4 the oldest; – is the oldest.
5 bigger; Yes, it is. / No, it isn't.
6 the nicest

8
more expensive than — the most expensive
more dangerous than — the most dangerous
better than — the best
worse than — the worst

10
more beautiful — the most beautiful
more expensive — the most expensive
more interesting — the most interesting
more exciting — the most exciting
more wonderful — the most wonderful

11
1 are more dangerous than; are the most dangerous
2 are more intelligent than, are the most intelligent
3 are more popular than; are the most popular
4 are more beautiful than; are the most beautiful
5 are more expensive than; are the most expensive
6 are better guard dogs than; are the best guard dogs

12
1 the quietest
2 more dangerous
3 smaller
4 cleaner
5 the noisiest
6 more intelligent
7 uglier
8 the best
9 the dirtiest
10 the most beautiful

13
(Students' own answers)

Unit 17

1
loud   loudly
quiet quietly
easy   easily

3
1 carefully
2 badly
3 well
4 fast
5 hard
6 slowly
7 quietly
8 neatly

4
Adjective	Adverb	Adjective or adverb
dangerous	funnily	fast
happy	perfectly	hard
lazy	safely	
nice	well	

5
1a carefully
1b careful
2a easy
2b easily
3a quiet
3b quietly
4a beautifully
4b beautiful
5a safe
5b safely

6
1 clumsy
2 hard
3 badly
4 well
5 carefully
6 quick
7 fast

7
1 Lucy is good at Art.
2 Peter sometimes works carelessly.
3 Harry and Beth always work hard.
4 English is easy.
5 Our teacher speaks clearly.
6 Beth is always polite.
7 Liz's mum always drives slowly.
8 Peter's room is very untidy.
9 I can't draw very well.
10 That story is very funny.

8
(Students' own answers)

Answer key

9
1. hard
2. beautiful
3. clearly
4. good
5. beautifully
6. great
7. clumsily
8. badly
9. funny

10
(Students' own answers)

Unit 18

1

I	am ('m)	going to play.
We/You/They	are ('re)	going to play.
He/She/It	is ('s)	going to play.

I	am not ('m not)	going to play.
We/You/They	are not (aren't)	going to play.
He/She/It	is not (isn't)	going to play.

Am	I	going to play?
Yes, I am.		
Are	we/you/they	going to play?
No, we/you/they aren't.		
Is	he/she/it	going to play?
Yes, he/she/it is.		

3
1. 's going to rain
2. 's going to fall
3. isn't going to win
4. 's going to be
5. 's going to drop
6. 's going to kick

4
1. 'm going to bring
2. 'm going to make
3. 's going to make
4. 'm not going to bring
5. 's not going to come
6. 's going to drive

5
1. Is she going to visit; Yes, she is.
2. Is she going to finish; No, she isn't.
3. Is she going to buy; Yes, she is.
4. Is she going to meet; Yes, she is.
5. Is she going to have; No, she isn't
6. Is she going to study; Yes, she is.
7. Is she going to go; No, she isn't.

6
1. are you going to do; 'm going to go; are you going to see; 're going to see
2. 's going to visit; is she going to stay; are you going to do; 're going to go
3. Are you going to go; 'm going to go; are you going to stay; aren't going to stay; 're going to go

7
1. What are you going to do at the weekend?
2. Are you going to stay at home?
3. What time are you going to stay up on Saturday?
4. Is your best friend going to visit you on Sunday?
5. Where are you going to go on holiday?
6. Are you going to have a party on your birthday?

8
Peter and I are going to paint the stalls.
Kevin and Diana are going to sell second-hand books.
Brian and Tina and going to make paper kites.
Tom is going to bring the sound system.
Vicky and Brian are going to play music.
Alex is going to sell drinks and food.
The whole class is going to clean up after the fair.

9
(Students' own answers)

Unit 19

1
No, I/he/she/it/we/you/they won't
I/You/He/She/It/We/You/They will not (won't) help.

3
(Students' own opinions)
1. will / won't
2. will / won't
3. will / won't
4. will / won't
5. will / won't
6. will / won't
7. will / won't
8. will / won't

🎧 38

4
1. Will I be; 'll have
2. Will people like; they will; 'll love
3. Will my friends laugh; they won't; 'll be
4. Will I be; you won't; 'll have
5. Will people buy; they will; 'll buy

5
1. I'll come with you.
2. I'll meet you at six.
3. I'll call him now.
4. I'll ask her.
5. I won't buy it.
6. I'll get my umbrella.

🎧 39

6
1. 'll be
2. won't
3. 'll be
4. 'll have
5. 'll spend
6. won't let
7. 'll have
8. will Aunt Agatha play
9. will be
10. 'll stay

7
1. will be
2. There will be
3. there will be
4. There won't be
5. will have
6. will live and work
7. will be
8. will have
9. won't be
10. will still be

🎧 40

8
1. I'll study
2. are you going to do
3. 's going to study
4. 'm not going to start
5. 'll visit
6. Are you going to go
7. are going to become
8. 're going to play

9
1 b	5 a
2 a	6 b
3 c	7 a
4 a	

10
(Students' own answers)

Use your English 4

🎧 41

1

Audioscript

1
A: Is this a photo of your family, Chris?
B: Yes, it's from our last summer holiday. Look – that's my dad. He's the one with the big sunglasses. Mum hates them. She says they are the biggest sunglasses in the whole world!
A: What's your dad's name?
B: Peter.

2
B: That's Michael.
A: Who's Michael?
B: He's my youngest cousin. Actually, he's the youngest in our family. He's only five months old!

17

Grammar Time 3

3
A: Who's the oldest person in your family?
B: I think it's my granny. She's in the photo, too. There she is. Her name's Sara.

4
A: Is that your sister, next to you?
B: No, my sister's taking the photograph. That's my other cousin, Emma. She's older than I am but she is shorter, too. The tall girl, next to Emma is her sister, Ruth.

5
A: There are two boys running in the background. Do you know them?
B: Yes, we stayed at the same hotel. They're twins. The one in the front is James and the other one is Tom.
A: How can you tell who is who?
B: James was always faster than Tom!

2
1 the youngest
2 the oldest
3 taller than
4 older than
5 faster than
6 the biggest

3
1 slowly
2 quickly
3 carefully
4 fast
5 safely
6 beautiful
7 well
8 good
9 bad
10 clearly

4
1 –   7 –
2 a   8 –
3 the   9 a
4 –   10 an
5 the   11 a
6 –   12 The

5
(Suggested answers)
1 It's going to rain.
2 I'm going to study / pass / fail.
3 I'm going to watch the film on TV.
4 She's going to do some exercise / join a gym.
5 I'm going to buy him a present.
6 I'm going to make a cake.

6
1 I'll help you!
2 I'll come with you.
3 I'll have a sandwich.
4 I won't buy it.
5 I'll wear my hat.

Unit 20

1

I/We/You/They	have ('ve)	made
He/She/It	has ('s)	packed

I/We/You/They	have not (haven't)	put
He/She/It	has not (hasn't)	eaten

Have	I/we/you/they made?
No,	I/we/you/they haven't.
Has	he/she/it packed?
Yes,	he/she/it has.

3
1 stopped
2 met
3 found
4 fed
5 said
6 brought
7 broken
8 written
9 seen
10 read
11 cut
12 put

4
1 b   4 f
2 d   5 e
3 c   6 a

5
1 has bought
2 has borrowed
3 has given
4 have downloaded
5 have said
6 haven't phoned
7 haven't packed
8 haven't made

6
1 Have you done
2 Has the rain stopped? No, it hasn't.
3 Has Emma bought; Yes, she has.
4 Have Tim and Alex met; Yes, they have.
5 Has Mike left; No, he hasn't.
6 Have you had; No, I haven't.

7
1 have you brought
2 has he bought
3 has
4 's put
5 've brought
6 have you made
7 have
8 's left
9 's taken

9
1 've just broken
2 has just moved
3 've just heard
4 's just eaten
5 've just read
6 've just bought
7 's just phoned
8 've just seen
9 've just come
10 have just bought

10
1 I haven't asked her yet.
2 I haven't had lunch yet.
3 We haven't seen it yet.
4 He hasn't gone to bed yet.
5 They haven't come back yet.
6 I haven't phoned her yet
7 I haven't started it yet.
8 They haven't gone home yet.

11
1 Peter's already done his homework.
2 He hasn't tidied his room yet.
3 He's already phoned Harry.
4 He hasn't fed Cosmo and Bella yet.
5 He hasn't found his football boots yet.
6 He's already read his History book.

12
1 Has Lucy bought …yet; Yes, she has.
2 Has she finished … yet; Yes, she has.
3 Has she sent … yet; No, she hasn't.
4 Has she told … yet; No, she hasn't.
5 Has she watched Nature Notes on TV yet; Yes, she has.
6 Has she made a cake for Dad yet; No, she hasn't.

13
(Possible answers)
1 Have you done your homework yet?
2 Have you washed the dishes yet?
3 Have you fed the cat/dog/bird yet?
4 Have you cleaned your room yet?
5 Have you bought tickets for the concert yet?
6 Have you downloaded any new songs yet?

14
1 have
2 seen / visited
3 met
4 's
5 had / eaten
6 already
7 bought
8 have
9 Have
10 yet

Answer key

15
1. Has Harry been; Yes, he has.
2. Has Harry visited … yet; No, he hasn't.
3. Has Harry been … yet; Yes, he has.
4. Has Harry bought … yet; Yes, he has.
5. Has Harry taken … yet; No, he hasn't.
6. Has Harry written … yet; Yes, he has.

16
(Students' own answers)

Unit 21

1
I've visited a theme park.
I haven't ever visited a theme park.

3
1. Harry hasn't been camping.
2. Beth hasn't lit a fire.
3. Peter and Lucy have slept in a tent.
4. Harry has swum in a river.
5. Beth has cooked food on a fire.
6. Peter and Lucy haven't swum in a river.
7. I haven't/have been camping.
8. I haven't/have slept in a tent.

4
1. Has … ever swum; Yes, he has.
2. Has … ever been; Yes, she has.
3. Have … ever slept; Yes, they have.
4. Has … ever lit; No, he hasn't.
5. Has … ever cooked; Yes, she has.
6. Have … ever swum; No, they haven't.
7. Have … cooked; Yes, I have. / No, I haven't.
8. Have you … slept; Yes, I have. / No, I haven't.

5
1. I've never been on TV.
2. My dad's never tried Mexican food.
3. My best friend has never played chess.
4. My brother has never seen a dolphin.
5. My parents have never been to Spain.
6. I've never climbed a mountain.
7. My friends and I have never flown in a helicopter.
8. My grandmother has never used computer.

6
1. Have you ever visited Disneyland?
2. Have you ever won a prize?
3. Have you ever been to another country?
4. Have you ever met a famous person?
5. Have your parents ever taken you to a theme park?
6. Has your mum ever ridden a horse?
7. Has your best friend ever sent you a postcard from another country?
8. Have you ever stayed in a hotel?

7
1. Have you read
2. haven't
3. 've never heard
4. Have you ever seen
5. have
6. Have you ever visited
7. haven't
8. 've never downloaded

8
1. has won
2. has never swum
3. has climbed
4. has never climbed
5. have been
6. have never been
7. has flown
8. has never driven
9. have ridden
10. have ridden

9
(Students' own answers)

Unit 22

1
I/He/She/It/We/You/They cannot (can't) play the piano
Can I/he/she/it/we/you/they play the piano?
No, I/he/she/it/we/you/they can't.
Could I/he/she/it/we/you/they play the piano?
No, I/he/she/it/we/you/they couldn't.

3
1. Can   5. can't
2. can't   6. can
3. can't   7. Can
4. Can, can't   8. can't

4
1. couldn't
2. Could
3. could
4. couldn't
5. could
6. Could
7. could
8. couldn't

5
1. could
2. Could
3. couldn't
4. can
5. couldn't
6. can't
7. can't
8. Can
9. can't
10. couldn't

6
1. You can use your dictionaries.
2. You can't open your books.
3. You can write with a pen or a pencil.
4. You can take notes.
5. You can't leave the classroom.
6. You can't speak to each other.
7. You can't show your answers to another student.
8. You can ask your teacher for help.

7
1. can
2. can't
3. can
4. Can
5. can
6. can
7. Can
8. can't
9. can
10. can't

8
The cats must not (mustn't) come into the house.
He/She/It has to go out.
He/She/It does not / doesn't have to go out.
Does he/she/it have to go out?
No, I/you/we/they don't.
Yes, he/she/it does.

10
1. mustn't   4. mustn't
2. must   5. must
3. must   6. mustn't

11
1. have to get up
2. don't have to wait
3. has to finish
4. have to be
5. don't have to take
6. don't have to stay
7. have to clean
8. don't have to go
9. doesn't have to buy
10. Do we have to do; we do
11. Does your mum have to work
12. Do you have to finish; I don't

12
1. must
2. Can
3. can't

Grammar Time 3

4 have
5 don't
6 Do
7 don't
8 can

13
1 can
2 have
3 can
4 don't
5 to
6 have
7 has
8 do
9 can
10 be/get

14
(Students' own answers)

Unit 23

1
You shouldn't spend all your money on CDs.
I'll help you.
Shall I make the sandwiches?
Would you like to have lunch now?

3
1 should
2 shouldn't
3 should
4 shouldn't
5 should
6 should

4
1 You should work harder.
2 You shouldn't stay up late tonight.
3 You should take some aspirin.
4 You should apologise to her.
5 You should ask your teacher to help you.
6 You shouldn't eat so much sugar.

5
1 Shall I
2 I'll
3 Shall I
4 I'll
5 Shall I
6 Shall I
7 I'll
8 I'll

6
1 Shall we
2 Let's
3 Would you like
4 Let's
5 Would you like
6 Shall we

7 Let's
8 Would you like

7
1 I'll
2 shouldn't
3 Let's
4 Would
5 Shall we
6 Let's
7 I'll
8 should I
9 shouldn't
10 I'll

8
1 I'll help
2 should see
3 Let's buy
4 Shall … ride
5 Let's have
6 shouldn't watch
7 Shall … answer

9
1 Would you like to drink something?
2 Shall I go out and buy some?
3 You should sit down, then.
4 Let's watch a DVD.
5 I'll make some.
6 Shall we watch something else?

Unit 24

1
We/You/They were not sleeping.
(weren't)

Was I/he/she/it swimming?
Yes, I/he/she/it was.
Were you/we/they sleeping?
No, you/we/they weren't.

3
1 was washing
2 wasn't doing
3 were talking
4 wasn't listening
5 was making
6 was chasing

4
1 What were you doing at lunch time yesterday?
 I was …
2 Was your family having dinner at eight o'clock last night?
 Yes, we were. / No, we weren't.
3 Were you doing your homework at half past six on Sunday?
 Yes, I was. / No, I wasn't.
4 Who were you talking to before class today?
 I was talking to …
5 What were you watching on TV last night?
 I was watching …
6 Was it raining at nine o'clock this morning?
 Yes, it was. / No, it wasn't.

5
He was carrying a bowl …
They were going home …
It was snowing …

While we were watching TV, …
While he was tidying his room, …

7
1 were watching
2 found
3 started
4 came
5 was getting
6 saw
7 was sleeping
8 was waiting

8
1 phoned, was studying
2 were cleaning, knocked
3 was raining, went
4 saw, were playing
5 walked, was listening
6 got up, were having
7 was waiting, saw
8 were having, rang

10
1 when
2 While
3 While
4 when
5 when
6 While

11
1 was reading, heard
2 were swimming, started
3 was getting, phoned
4 were shopping, saw
5 were driving, stopped
6 found, was tidying
7 were playing, arrived
8 was having, arrived

12
1 were
2 when
3 you
4 was
5 were
6 Was
7 when
8 was
9 did
10 What
11 was
12 when
13 Was
14 wasn't
15 Did
16 Yes

20

Answer key

13
1. were playing
2. went
3. sat
4. was carrying
5. started
6. was running

14
1. were playing a computer game
2. came into the room
3. was putting the sandwiches on a plate
4. was getting some orange juice
5. were washing our hands
6. was eating one of the sandwiches
7. was laughing
8. jumped on the table

Unit 25

1
1. Has
2. Were
3. Are
4. Have
5. Could
6. Were

3
1. Is
2. Is
3. Can
4. Could
5. Were
6. Should
7. Have
8. Will
9. Have

4
1. Did; did
2. Do; do
3. Does; doesn't
4. Did; didn't
5. Do; don't
6. Does; doesn't

5
1. Have you got a computer?
2. Do you and your family live in London?
3. Have you ever ridden a camel?
4. Are you going to play tennis on Saturday?
5. Did your dad go to work yesterday?
6. Was it raining last weekend?

6
1. What
2. Where
3. Whose
4. How
5. many

8
1. What
2. Who
3. How much
4. Where

5. When
6. How many
7. Why
8. Whose

9
1. milk have we got
2. are you crying
3. is that / he
4. are they doing/drinking
5. is Cosmo
6. bag is that
7. do you visit your grandparents / cousins / friends
8. money have you got

10
1. How does this camera work? – e
2. What should I do? – c
3. Where were they going? – g
4. When did the film start? – a
5. Why is Tessa running? – f
6. How many CDs did you buy? – d
7. Whose bag is that? – b

🎧 52
11
1. Who's that girl
2. What's her name
3. Where does she come from
4. Can she speak English
5. Where does she live
6. How many brothers or sisters has she got
7. Why does she never talk

12
1. you
2. they
3. was
4. they
5. is
6. will
7. have
8. can

14
1. isn't it
2. didn't they
3. don't you
4. can't she
5. weren't they
6. couldn't he
7. aren't I
8. haven't we
9. haven't you
10. shouldn't I

15
1. you
2. has he
3. do you
4. is it
5. could she
6. isn't it
7. did she
8. are you

🎧 53
16
1. don't you
2. have you
3. aren't we
4. haven't you
5. isn't it

17
(Students' own answers)

Use your English 5

1

Audioscript

1
A: Have you ever been to a foreign country, Mark?
B: Yes, I have. I've already visited six countries.
A: Have you been to Asia, too?
B: Yes, I have! I've been to China!

2
A: Hello.
B: Hi, Anna! How are you?
A: Not very well…
B: Why? What's happened?
A: I've broken my leg.
B: Oh, no! Does it hurt?
A: A little bit…

3
A: Jenny! I'm home! (door closes) Where are you?
B: In the kitchen, Mum!
A: Something smells great! What is it?
B: Look! I've made a cake.
A: Darling, it looks wonderful!

4
A: My dad was a pilot, you know, Patricia.
B: What about you? Can you fly a plane?
A: No, I'm afraid I can only drive a car.
B: I can fly a plane.
A: Really? That's brilliant!
B: I've only flown three times alone, though.

5
A: Can you ride, uncle David?
B: Mmm
A: Have you ever ridden an elephant?
B: No, but I've ridden a camel!

6
A: It's your mum's birthday tomorrow, Tom.
B: Yes, dad. I know.
A: I don't know what to get her. Do you?
B: I'm ready. I've already bought her a present.
A: What is it?
B: I'm not telling you. It's a surprise.

21

Grammar Time 3

Mark – d
Anna – a
Jenny – b
Patricia – f
David – c
Tom – e

2
1 Mark has visited
2 Anna has broken
3 Jenny has made
4 Patricia has flown
5 David has ridden
6 Tom has bought

3
1 must
2 mustn't
3 don't have to
4 can
5 mustn't / can't
6 don't have to
7 can
8 can
9 mustn't / can't

4
1 Is it on your desk?
2 You should ask Mum. Maybe she's seen it.
3 You haven't finished your homework, yet, have you?
4 Great. Let's watch a DVD, then.
5 Shall I go to the DVD rental shop?
6 What would you like to watch?

5
1 called
2 was drying
3 did you do
4 Did you go
5 were playing
6 started
7 were washing
8 began

Key to the Photocopiable Quizzes

Quiz 1

A
1 b   4 b
2 a   5 a
3 b   6 a

B
1 How   4 your
2 old   5 best
3 is   6 friend

C
How old is your best friend?
My best friend is …

D
1 b   4 b
2 b   5 a
3 a   6 b

E
1 an
2 the
3 the
4 an
5 the

Quiz 2

A
1 friend's
2 boys'
3 shoes
4 sister's
5 brothers'
6 children's

B
1 walls
2 name
3 top
4 end
5 capital
6 back

C
1 have   4 No
2 got   5 They
3 has   6 have

D
1 mine
2 hers
3 Whose
4 yours
5 his
5 Theirs

Quiz 3

A
1 a   4 b
2 a   5 b
3 a

B

C
(Students' own answers)

D
1 Is
2 it
3 a
4 cinema
5 in
6 your
7 town

E
Is there a cinema in your town?
Yes, there is. / No, there isn't.

Quiz 4

A
1 them   4 me
2 him   5 we
3 us   6 her

B
1 time
2 What
3 you
4 they
5 times / days
6 on

C
1 b   4 a
2 b   5 b
3 a   6 a

D
1 I often meet my friends in the park.
2 I sometimes watch TV in the morning.
3 I play football three times a week.
4 I always go to bed early on Sundays.
5 My mum usually goes shopping on Fridays.
6 We never go to the cinema at the weekend.

Quiz 5

A
1 are staying
2 It's
3 writing
4 watching
5 are
6 is
7 am wearing
8 you doing

B
1 'm staying
2 washes
3 is washing
4 don't go
5 isn't raining

Answer key

C
1 a   4 a
2 b   5 b
3 b   6 b

D
1 is very good exercise
2 visit France
3 going to restaurants
4 good for you
5 in visiting museums
6 with playing computer games

Quiz 6

A
1 no
2 a lot
3 some
4 any
5 any
6 no

B
1 nothing
2 anything
3 someone
4 anywhere
5 something
6 no-one

C
1 How
2 many
3 people
4 live
5 in
6 your
7 house

D
How many people live in your house?
… people live in my house.

E
1 bread   3 pizza
2 water   4 cola

Quiz 7

A
1 were
2 Was
3 was
4 were
5 were

B
1 Were
2 you
3 at
4 school
5 yesterday
6 afternoon

C
Were you at school yesterday afternoon?
Yes, I was. / No, I wasn't.

D
1 Did you go
2 didn't
3 stayed
4 made
5 did you make
6 painted
7 went
8 bought
9 Did you walk
10 didn't
11 took

Quiz 8

A
1 the   4 an
2 a   5 the
3 the   6 –

B
1 b   4 b
2 a   5 a
3 a   6 a

C
1 more interesting than
2 the most popular
3 bigger
4 stronger
5 better
6 the worst

D
1 clearly
2 easily
3 fast
4 badly
5 polite
5 easy

Quiz 9

A
1 going   4 not
2 not   5 is
3 are   6 are

B
1 a present for my mum
2 do at the weekend?
3 going to visit her uncle on Saturday?
4 going to rain
5 to go to the hairdresser's
6 aren't going to have a party on their birthday

C
1 I hope our team will win.
2 I think you'll be a famous artist.
3 I hope Aunt Agatha won't play the piano.
4 It won't be busy on the beach today.
5 What will you do after school?
6 There will be a hotel here in ten years' time.

D
1 go
2 work
3 have
4 cook
5 come
6 be

Quiz 10

A
1 Yes, he has.
2 Yes, she has.
3 No, she hasn't.
4 Yes, they have.
5 No, he hasn't.
6 No, she hasn't.

B
1 done   4 have
2 tidied   5 read
3 washed   6 put

C
1 Have you ever been to Australia?
2 Has your mum ever driven a bus?
3 Has Harry ever slept in a tent?
4 Have you ever seen a dolphin?
5 Has your dad ever made a pizza?
6 Have your friends ever tried Chinese food?

D
1 just
2 yet
3 never
4 just
5 already
6 never

Quiz 11

A
1 can't use
2 could ride
3 can't find
4 can't drive
5 can speak
6 Can I borrow
7 can, couldn't swim

B
1 doesn't
2 has
3 must
4 mustn't
5 mustn't
6 have

Grammar Time 3

C
1 b
2 a
3 a
4 a
5 b

D
1 to eat something
2 when you were little?
3 a present for our teacher?
4 my teacher about this?
5 your letter for you?
6 a question?

Quiz 12

A
1 When
2 was
3 when
4 What
5 was
6 were

B
1 b
2 a
3 a
4 b
5 a

C
1 have you?
2 can't you?
3 doesn't she?
4 did you?
5 aren't I?

D
1 What
2 is
3 the
4 capital
5 of
6 your
7 country

E
What is the capital of your country?
The capital of my country is …

Use your English (Units 1–5)

A
1 are
2 is
3 are
4 are
5 are
6 is
7 are
8 is
9 am

B
1 feet
2 friends
3 leaf
4 person
5 women

C
1 This
2 that
3 those
4 is
5 an

D
1 uncle's
2 parents'
3 children's
4 Lucy's
5 brothers'
6 friend's
7 men's
8 girls'
9 Charles' or Charles's

E
1 has
2 Has
3 haven't
4 have
5 has

F
1 Whose
2 mine
3 your
4 my
5 yours

G
1 opposite
2 behind
3 on
4 under
5 between

H
1 Is there …; No, there isn't.
2 Are there …; Yes, there are.
3 Are there …; No, there aren't.
4 Is there …; Yes, there is.
5 Is there …; No, there isn't.

Use your English (Units 6–10)

A
1 Let's
2 Don't
3 Let's
4 Let's
5 Don't

B
1 her
2 them
3 him
4 it
5 me

C
1 visits
2 on
3 doesn't
4 in
5 goes

6 at
7 hates
8 tidy
9 on

D
1 Do Cosmo and Bella often have milk? Yes, they do.
2 Does Harry always get up late? No, he doesn't.
3 Does Beth usually walk to school? Yes, she does.
4 Does Harry often watch TV? Yes, he does.
5 Does Beth sometimes get up late? No, she doesn't.
6 Do Cosmo and Bella always get up early? No, they don't.

E
1 watch
2 are watching
3 aren't going
4 Does Harry tidy
5 I'm working
6 Do you brush
7 have
8 Is the baby sleeping
9 is wearing
10 don't have

F
1 to go
2 skiing
3 Dancing
4 visiting
5 playing
6 to wear
7 to be
8 shopping
9 to visit
10 going

Use your English (Units 11–15)

A
1 Countable
2 Uncountable
3 Countable
4 Uncountable

B
1 any
2 any
3 someone
4 anywhere
5 some
6 anyone
7 some
8 no
9 any

C
1 many
2 many
3 a lot of

Answer key

4 much
5 many
6 much
7 much
8 a lot of
9 a lot of

D
1 soup
2 pizza
3 water
4 bread
5 milk

E
1 Were
2 weren't
3 was
4 Was
5 were
6 were
7 weren't
8 wasn't
9 were

F
1 saw
2 finished
3 bought
4 had
5 visited
6 wrote
7 went
8 found
9 played

Use your English (Units 16–20)

A
1 more
2 biggest
3 more
4 beautiful
5 than
6 worst
7 most
8 older
9 oldest

B
1 well
2 badly
3 fast
4 hard
5 quickly

C
1a carefully
1b careful
2a polite
2b politely
3a beautiful
3b beautifully
4a noisy
4b noisily

5a easy
5b easily

D
1 going
2 am
3 are
4 play
5 it's
6 are
7 go
8 Are
9 not

E
1 I hope our team will win.
2 There will be lots of people at the beach today.
3 I think I'll stay in this evening.
4 Will there be cities on Mars in fifty years' time?
5 Will you help me tidy my room?
6 Our town will be different in twenty years' time.
7 Will Lucy be a famous artist?
8 It will be boring at Aunt Agatha's.
9 There won't be many people at the party.
10 Mum won't let us stay up late this evening.

F
1 -
2 the
3 -
4 -
5 a
6 an
7 the
8 an
9 a

Use your English (Units 21–25)

1 've cleaned
2 has made
3 has bought
4 've borrowed
5 've phoned
6 have eaten
7 has broken

B
1 yet
2 already
3 just
4 never
5 has
6 ever
7 haven't

C
1 has to
2 must
3 Can
4 couldn't
5 Could
6 have to
7 mustn't

D
1 shouldn't
2 should
3 should
4 shouldn't
5 should

E
1 Shall we
2 Let's
3 Would you like
4 Would you like
5 Shall we
6 Would you like
7 Let's

F
1 was reading
2 heard
3 was snowing
4 got up
5 saw
6 was waiting
7 walked
8 were dancing

G
1 can't
2 Why
3 Could
4 Did
5 isn't
6 aren't
7 Which

25

Grammar Time 3

Teacher's notes for photocopiable activity sheets

Teacher's notes for photocopiable activity sheets

Unit 1

Preparation: Photocopy one activity sheet for every pupil in the class.

1 Make pairs. Use one word from A and one word from B.

- Use the example of *school magazine* to show pupils how they can make compound nouns by choosing a word from box A and another from box B. Tell them that all the compounds are to be found in Unit 1. The only exception is *Grammar Time*, which should be recognisable.
- Pupils may work individually or in pairs.

Answers
school magazine   Grammar Time
football team   best friend
birthday party   living room

2 Write the words under the correct heading.

- Pupils must sort the words into the five categories shown. Use the examples – *short*, *fish*, etc. – to ensure that pupils understand the meaning of each category. You can drawn five columns on the board and give further examples for each category, to ensure that pupils understand the task: *old, horse, mother, Greece, Music, …*
- Revise the English name of your pupils' country, if this does not appear in the exercise.

Answers
Adjectives: short, new, tall, thirsty, hungry
Animals: fish, cat, dog, mouse, snake
People: friend, brother, neighbour, sister, student
Countries: Italy, China, England, Spain, Turkey
Subjects: Science, Geography, History, Maths, English

Unit 2

Preparation: Photocopy one activity sheet for every pupil in the class.

1 Find five sentences.

- Beginning with the words in circles, pupils must find five sentences by moving up or down, left or right. One sentence is given as an example.
- Pupils should work in pencil, so that they can correct mistakes.

Answers
My sister is very tall.
Is that your dog?
My room isn't very big.
These are the photos from the picnic.
Cosmo and Bella are Harry's cats.

2 Unjumble this sentence.

- Pupils must put the words in order to create a sentence they have read in Unit 2.

Answer
These are the photos from Sarah's birthday party.

3 Write a jumbled sentence for your partner. Use a sentence from Unit 2.

- Pupils can refer to their Pupils' Book and create their own jumbled sentences for their friends to re-order.
- If you have enough time, invite pupils to come and write their jumbled sentences on the board and try to unscramble them yourself. Children enjoy playing the role of the teacher from time to time.

Unit 3

Preparation: Photocopy one activity sheet for every pupil in the class.

1 Find and write.

- Use the illustration of the five children for questions around the class. Hold up your copy of the worksheet, point to the children and ask:

What's her/his name? What has she/he got? Has she/he got glasses? … a cat? … a dog? … an umbrella? etc. *What's she/he wearing? Is she/he wearing a T-shirt? … shorts?* etc.
- Pupils look at the ten small pictures and decide who each item belongs to by referring to the main picture. They then write captions to the pictures, using the possessive *–'s*

Answers
1 Helen's bag
2 Sarah's shoes
3 Charles' T-shirt
4 David's dog
5 Fred's hat
6 Helen's glasses
7 Sarah's umbrella
8 Charles' shoes
9 David's feet
10 Fred's feet

2 Match.

- The activity focuses on the noun phrases with *of* presented on page 16 of the Pupils' Book. Pupils draw linking lines to make complete sentences.

Answers
1 There's a swimming pool at the back of our school.
2 The end of this film is very funny.
3 There are two birds on the roof of that house.
4 Madrid is the capital of Spain.
5 I don't like the colour of this T-shirt.
6 There's a little house on the top of that mountain.

Unit 4

Preparation: Photocopy one activity sheet for every pupil in the class. Cut each sheet in half along the dotted line.

1 Ask and answer to complete the table. Write [✓] or [✗].

- If your class is unfamiliar with information-gap activities, take some time to explain the procedure. Ask two confident pupils to come to the front of the class and demonstrate the activitiy. Once the class have understood the activity, they will be able to begin future pairwork activities with less rehearsing.

- Divide the class into A/B pairs. Give copies of sheets A and B to each pair. In their pairs, pupils ask questions to complete the table.
- If possible, arrange for pupils to sit facing each other, rather than side-by-side. This will prevent them looking at their friend's sheet and create a true information gap.
- Circulate and ensure that pupils are using the singular and plural forms of *have got* correctly.

2 Write sentences.

- Pupils write sentences using the information they obtained in Exercise 1.

Answers
A
1 Fred's mum and dad have got a car.
2 Helen's got a dog.
3 Fred's mum and dad have got a computer.
4 Fred hasn't got a computer.
5 Helen's mum and dad haven't got a car.

B
1 Helen's mum and dad have got a cat.
2 Helen hasn't got a cat.
3 Fred's mum and dad have got a car.
4 Fred hasn't got a dog.
5 Helen's mum and dad haven't got a computer.

Unit 5

Preparation: Photocopy one activity sheet for every pupil in the class.

1 Read and draw.

- If necessary, revise the prepositions shown on page 24 of the Pupils' Book.
- Hand out the worksheets. Pupils read the caption for each picture and complete it, as instructed.

2 Read the clues and complete the grid. Find the mystery word.

- As pupils complete the six horizontal words in the grid, the six letters of the mystery word – written vertically – will be revealed.
- Depending on your class, you may wish to do the activity orally first and establish the answers to the six clues. Do not let pupils write during this preparation phase.

Grammar Time 3

Answers
1 magazine
2 because
3 sandwich
4 laptop
5 at
6 toothbrush
The mystery word is *guitar*.

Unit 6

Preparation: Photocopy one activity sheet for every pupil in the class.

1 Make and say sentences. Work in pairs and take turns.

- Before pupils begin work on the activity sheet, write on the board *Where's my pen? I can't find it*. Have the class repeat the sentences after you. Rub out *my pen* and substitute a name, e.g. Maria or the name of a pupil in the class. Say *Where's Maria? I can't find —* and elicit the object pronoun *her*.
- Continue in the same way with a boy's name, to elicit the pronoun *him*.
- Continue with a plural example, e.g. my keys. Point again to the sentences on the board, and ask pupils what needs to change: *Where are my keys? I can't find them*.
- For further reinforcement, read nouns from the list on the worksheet – *Lucy?* etc. – and have pupils give the full question: *Where's Lucy? I can't find her*.
- Hand out the activity sheet. Ask pupils to work in pairs and make questions like the one you wrote on the board. They must choose the correct words from each list. They can take turns to make questions, correcting each other's choices where necessary.

2 Write sentences from Exercise 1.

- Working alone, pupils write some of the sentences they created in Exercise 1.

Answers
Where's Lucy? I can't find her.
Where are my keys? I can't find them.
Where's my book? I can't find it.
Where are Cosmo and Bella? I can't find them.
Where's Harry? I can't find him.
Where's my football? I can't find it.
Where are Mum's photos? I can't find them.
Where are my glasses? I can't find them.
Where are my jeans? I can't find them.
Where's my homework? I can't find it.
Where's Aunt Agatha? I can't find her.
Where's the birthday cake? I can't find it.
Where's Dad? I can't find him.
Where's my football? I can't find it.
Where's the museum? I can't find it.
Where are my new shoes? I can't find them.

Unit 7

Preparation: Photocopy one activity sheet for every pupil in the class. Cut each sheet in half along the dotted line.

1 Ask and answer to complete the text.

- Divide the class into A/B pairs. If possible, arrange the class so that pupils are sitting opposite their pairwork partner. Give copies of sheets A and B to each pair.
- Pupils take turns to ask their partner a question, in order to complete the gaps in the information about David and Fred. They should use the question words shown in speech bubbles at the bottom of the sheet.
- Depending on your class, you may wish to go through the questions orally before pupils work in pairs. If so, hand out only the A-sheets and ask pupils to share them. Rehearse the questions, but do not give answers. Then hand out the B-sheets and let pupils work in pairs.

Unit 8

Preparation: Photocopy one activity sheet for every pupil in the class.

1 Choose the correct word.

- Pupils read the boy's description of his normal Sunday routine, and circle the correct word.

Answers
1 usually
2 never
3 often
4 go
5 read
6 at
7 Sometimes
8 In

2 Find and underline one answer which is not possible.

- For each of A's questions, there are two possible correct answers and one which is not possible. Pupils must identify the impossible answer and underline it, as in the example.

Answers
1 Yes, I do.
2 At seven o'clock.
3 No, I don't.
4 No, I don't. I never go to the cinema.
5 Yes, I do. I always get up at seven o'clock.
6 No, I don't.

Unit 9

Preparation: Photocopy one activity sheet for every pupil in the class.

1 Find six sentences.

- Beginning with the words in circles, pupils must find five sentences by moving up or down, left or right. One sentence is given as an example.
- Pupils should work in pencil, so that they can correct mistakes.

Answers
I'm studying English at the moment.
I play football every day.
We always have lunch at twelve o'clock.
My brother is doing his homework right now.
Our teacher plays tennis once a week.
My cousin is staying with us this week.

2 Unjumble this sentence.

- Pupils must put the words in order to create a sentence they have read in Unit 9.

Answer
We always have a party on your birthday.

3 Write a jumbled sentence for your friend. Use a sentence from Unit 9.

- Pupils can refer to their Pupils' Book and create their own jumbled sentences for their friends to re-order.
- If you have enough time, invite pupils to come and write their jumbled sentences on the board and try to unscramble them yourself.

Children enjoy playing the role of the teacher from time to time.

Unit 10

Preparation: Photocopy one activity sheet for every pupil in the class.

1 Choose the true answer.

- Pupils read the questions and circle the reply which is true for them. Depending on your class, you may wish to go through the exercise orally first. Encourage pupils to use short answers.

2 Ask two friends. Write [✔] or [X].

- Pupils' answers to Exercise 1 will allow them to complete the table in Exercise 2. Each pupil must choose two classmates and ask them the six questions about their tastes and aspirations. They write their classmates' names at the top of the column, then record their answers, using ticks and crosses.
- Insist on short answers throughout.

3 Write about your friends.

- Working individually, pupils write sentences reflecting the answers their classmates gave them in Exercise 2.

Unit 11

Preparation: Photocopy one activity sheet for every pupil in the class.

1 Look and correct the sentences.

- Ensure pupils understand that each of the seven sentences about the picture is incorrect. Their task is to look at the picture then write a correct version of the each sentence, as in the example.

Answers
1 There's some fruit in the bowl.
2 There aren't any sandwiches in the fridge.
3 There is some milk in the fridge.
4 There are two/some bananas in the bowl.
5 There's one cake in the fridge.
6 There aren't any eggs in the fridge.
7 There are two oranges in the bowl.

Grammar Time 3

2 Write the words under the correct heading. Then find them in the word square.

- Pupils write the words under the correct heading, then find and circle them in the word square. Words read horizontally from left to right, vertically from top to bottom, but not diagonally or backwards.
- Tell the class that the countable nouns are all written horizontally and the uncountable nouns are written vertically. This will allow them to check that their answers are correct.

Answers
Countable nouns: banana, biscuit, bottle, egg, pancake, sandwich
Uncountable nouns: cheese, chocolate, coffee, popcorn, water, yoghurt

```
N A H P E L E C T E G G
P A N C A K E H P F N A
C A L H E L T E O S C W
O O N O H T E E P B M A
F Y T C R B I S C U I T
F H G O U R O E O B Y E
E T G L N I N N R K O R
E N T A X I R B N N G O
B O T T L E K C O T H S
A H P E A L C L L E U W
O S A N D W I C H C R M
A B E B A N A N A Q T M
```

Unit 12

Preparation: Photocopy one activity sheet for every pupil in the class.

1 Match and make sentences.

- Pupils draw linking lines to make complete sentences.

Answers
1 There are a lot of people on the beach today.
2 There isn't much cheese on this pizza.
3 There are a lot of children in my class.
4 There aren't many shops near my school.
5 There aren't many biscuits in that packet.
6 There isn't much water in that bottle.

2 Read and write the children's names.

- The puzzle is intended to reactivate language from earlier units. Pupils look at the picture, read the sentences and work out the name of each of the eight children. They then write the names below the picture.

Answers
1 Sally   5 Nina
2 Jenny   6 Peter
3 Ben   7 Emma
4 Nick   8 Bill

Unit 13

Preparation: Photocopy one activity sheet for every pupil in the class.

1 Read and match.

- Pupils must read the clues and deduce where Sarah and her friends were yesterday afternoon.
- They should draw lines linking the faces to the places. Tell them to draw in pencil so that they can correct any mistakes.

Answers
Sarah – at the hairdresser's
David – at the cinema
Helen – at the cinema
Charles – at home
Fred – at Charles's house

2 Are these sentences true (T) or false (F)?

- The sentences refer to the children in Exercise 1. Pupils read the sentences and decide if they are true or false.

Answers
1 F   4 F
2 T   5 F
3 T   6 T

3 Write answers.

- Pupils answer the questions about the children in Exercise 1.

30

Answers
1 They were at Charles's house.
2 Charles.
3 David.
4 She was at the hairdresser's.
5 No, she wasn't.

Unit 14

Preparation: Photocopy one activity sheet for every pupil in the class.

1 Find six sentences in the Past simple.

- Beginning with the words in circles, pupils must find five sentences by moving up or down, left or right. One sentence is given as an example.
- Pupils should work in pencil, so that they can correct mistakes.

Answers
My dog ate my birthday cake!
We didn't go to the supermarket yesterday.
I saw a famous football player.
Lucy wrote a letter to her friend in Japan.
My dad bought some flowers for my mum.
He finished his homework an hour ago.

2 Unjumble this sentence.

- Pupils must put the words in order to create a sentence they have read in Unit 14.

Answer
Cosmo chewed the box and ate the cat food.

3 Write a jumbled sentence for your friend. Use a sentence from Unit 14.

- Pupils can refer to their Pupils' Book and create their own jumbled sentences for their friends to re-order.
- If you have enough time, invite pupils to come and write their jumbled sentences on the board and try to unscramble them yourself.

Unit 15

Preparation: Photocopy one activity sheet for every pupil in the class. Cut each sheet in half along the dotted line. Arrange the pupils in pairs. Give one pupil in each pair part A and the other, part B.

1 Complete the questions.

- In preparation for the information-gap activity which follows, pupils must choose the correct word to complete the question. Half the pupils will be completing questions about Helen. The others will complete the same questions, but about David.
- Correct the exercise orally with the class. Ask pupils to repeat each completed question.

Answers
1 subject   4 speak
2 favourite   5 country
3 food   6 want

2 & 3 Ask Student A/B questions from Exercise 1 to complete the information about David/Helen. Now answer Student A/B's questions about Helen/David.

- If possible, pupils should sit opposite their partner. First one pupil asks questions about Helen, and completes the sentences. Then the other pupil asks about David in the same way.

Unit 16

Preparation: Photocopy one activity sheet for every pupil in the class.

1 Look at the pictures and complete the grid. Find the mystery animal.

- Pupils must identify the nine animals in the pictures and write their names in the squares. As they complete the nine horizontal words, the nine letters of the mystery animal – written vertically – will be revealed.
- Depending on your class, you may wish to do the activity orally first and establish the answers to the nine clues. Do not let pupils write during this preparation phase.

Answers
1 cat   6 hamster
2 shark   7 iguana
3 horse   8 goldfish
4 parrot   9 alsatian

Grammar Time 3

> 5 snake
> The mystery animal is *tarantula*.

② Match.

- Pupils draw lines to link the two halves of each sentence. The activity tests their grasp of syntax, rather than their knowledge of natural history.

> **Answers**
> 1 Sharks are more dangerous than dolphins.
> 2 Hamsters are prettier than tarantulas.
> 3 Dogs are more expensive than hamsters.
> 4 Parrots are more intelligent than snakes.
> 5 Alsatians are stronger than poodles.
> 6 People are the most intelligent animals in the world.
> 7 Dogs are better pets than iguanas.

Unit 17

Preparation: Photocopy one activity sheet for every pupil in the class.

① Find and underline one answer which is not possible.

- Explain that two of the three answer choices are possible, but the other is grammatically incorrect.
- Pupils must identify and underline the word which is incorrect.

> **Answers**
> 1 bad   5 good
> 2 quick   6 safe
> 3 quietly   7 quickly
> 4 untidy   8 careful

② Play a guessing game.

- It will probably be best to play one or two rounds of the game with the class, by way of demonstration. Invite a volunteer to come to the front. Ask them to think of a famous person and whisper their name to you. This will allow you to guide their choice towards a celebrity class will know. Write the person's initials on the board.
- Help the rest of the class to ask questions, using the model shown on the activity sheet.

During this phase you can write further choices on the board: other professions (*athlete, comic, …*) and nationalities.

- Pupils then work in A/B pairs.
- A thinks of a famous person. (Encourage them to choose a living person – one whom all the class will know.) They write the initials of the person's name on a piece of paper, and show it to B.
- B must identify the person by asking the questions shown on the activity sheet. A can only answer *Yes, he/she is* or *No, he/she isn't*.

Unit 18

Preparation: Photocopy one activity sheet for every pupil in the class.

① Choose the correct word.

- Pupils complete the picture captions, choosing words from the box.

> **Answers**
> 1 take   4 going
> 2 is   5 wash
> 3 are   6 rain

② Now draw the pictures.

- Pupils do their own drawings to illustrate sentences 2-6. Remind them that they must show what is *going to* happen, not what is actually happening. So in picture 3, for example, some people must be *about* to fall into a swimming pool, the sea or wherever, but should *not* be actually in the water.

Unit 19

Preparation: Photocopy one activity sheet for every pupil in the class.

① Match the sentences with the pictures.

- Introduce the topic of the future. Say *Let's think about the future. What will people do? Will they have cars? Will there be schools and houses?* Introduce the question *Do you think* by asking different pupils *Do you think there will be cars?* etc.

Photocopiable activities

- Hand out the activity sheet. Focus on Exercise 1 and ensure that everyone understands the task. Give the class a few minutes to read the sentences and try to link them to the pictures.
- Read each sentence aloud and ask pupils to show you the matching picture.

Answers
1 d   4 a
2 b   5 e
3 f   6 c

2 Ask your friends. Write [✔] or [✗].

- Pupils work in groups of four. They should write their friends' names at the top of the columns.
- Demonstrate the activity by asking pupils *Do you think people won't read books?* etc. Insist on short answers: *Yes, I do* or *No, I don't*.
- Pupils take turns to ask their friends' opinions about the future, using *Do you think …* They record the answer by putting a tick or a cross under their friend's name.

3 Write about your friends.

- Pupils write sentences about what their friends have said, beginning *[Maria] thinks / doesn't think …*

Unit 20 & 21

Preparation: Photocopy one activity sheet for every pupil in the class.

1 Match. Then answer the questions for you. Write [✔] or [✗].

- Pupils draw linking lines to create questions in the present perfect.
- They give true answers by putting a tick or a cross in the *You* column. Demonstrate by asking one or two pupils *Have you ever fallen off your bike?* etc. Insist on short answers: *Yes, I have* or *No, I haven't*.

Answers
1 Have you ever fallen off your bike?
2 Have you ever eaten Chinese food?
3 Have you ever been to London?
4 Have you ever swum in the sea?
5 Have you ever broken your arm?
6 Have you ever seen a snake?
7 Have you ever been in an aeroplane?

2 Ask and answer the questions in Exercise 1.

- Pupils work in pairs, asking and answering the questions in Exercise 1. They record their partner's answers using ticks and crosses.

3 Write about you and your friend.

- Pupils write sentences about the questionnaire results, using the present perfect

Unit 22

Preparation: Photocopy one activity sheet for every pupil in the class.

1 Make and say rules for the class. Work in pairs and take turns.

- Hand out the activity sheet. Ask pupils to work in pairs and make rules for the classroom. They must choose the correct phrases from each list. They can take turns to make rules, correcting each other's choices where necessary.

2 Write your rules from Exercise 1.

- Working alone, pupils write some of the sentences they created in Exercise 1.

Answers (In any order:)
We must come to school every day.
We must do our homework.
We must listen to our teacher.
We must be polite.
We mustn't eat/run in the classroom.
We mustn't be late.
We mustn't listen to music.
We mustn't wear sunglasses in the classroom.
We don't have to come to school on Sundays.
We don't have to wear our best clothes.
We can run/talk to our friends in the playground.

Unit 23

Preparation: Photocopy one activity sheet for every pupil in the class.

Grammar Time 3

1 Find and underline one answer which is not possible.

- For each of A's questions, there are two possible correct answers and one which is not possible. Pupils must identify the impossible answer and underline it, as in the example.

Answers
1 That's a good idea.
2 Yes, you're right.
3 I'll show you.
4 Shall I give it to you?
5 You should see a dentist.
6 Thanks.

2 Read the clues and complete the grid. Find the mystery word.

- As pupils complete the eight horizontal words in the grid, the eight letters of the mystery word – written vertically – will be revealed.
- Depending on your class, you may wish to do the activity orally first and establish the answers to the eight clues.

Answers
1 difficult   5 sandwiches
2 toothache   6 carry
3 mustn't   7 headache
4 phone   8 tired
The mystery word is *lemonade*.

Unit 24

Preparation: Photocopy one activity sheet for every pupil in the class.

1 Read and match.

- Pupils must read the clues and deduce what Sarah and her friends were doing at six o'clock yesterday evening.
- They should draw lines linking the faces to the places. Tell them to draw in pencil so that they can correct any mistakes.

Answers
Sarah – playing volleyball
David – waiting for a bus
Helen – washing the car
Charles – making a model aeroplane
Fred – sleeping in the garden

2 Are these sentences true (T) or false (F)?

- The sentences refer to the children in Exercise 1. Pupils read the sentences and decide if they are true or false.

Answers
1 F   4 T
2 F   5 T
3 T   6 F

3 Write answers.

- Pupils answer the questions about the children in Exercise 1.

Answers
1 They were washing the car.
2 Sarah.
3 Yes, he was.
4 No, he wasn't.
5 He was sleeping.

Unit 25

Preparation: Photocopy one activity sheet for every pupil in the class.

1 Make and say questions in pairs.

- Hand out the activity sheet. Ask pupils to work in pairs and make questions. They must choose the correct phrases from each list. They can take turns to make questions, correcting each other's choices where necessary.

2 Write the questions from Exercise 1. Then answer the questions.

- Pupils write some of the questions they created in Exercise 1. They then write true answers.

Answers (In any order:)
What's your favourite colour?
Who's your favourite football player?
What time do you go to bed?
How often do you watch TV?
How many children are there in your class?
What's your teacher's name?
How old is your best friend?
Where do you live?
What are you going to do this evening?
When is your birthday?
Which child is the tallest in your class?

Photocopiable Activity Sheet

Unit 1

1 Make pairs. Use one word from A and one word from B.

A
football Grammar best birthday living school

B
friend room party magazine living team Time

school magazine
....
....
....
....
....

2 Write the words under the correct heading.

brother cat dog neighbour Spain China England History hungry fish friend Geography Italy Maths new short sister mouse English Science snake Turkey student tall thirsty

Adjectives	Animals	People	Countries	Subjects
short	fish	friend	Italy	Science
....	....	....	....	....
....	....	....	....	....
....	....	....	....	....
....	....	....	....	....

Photocopiable © Pearson Education Limited 2008

Grammar Time 3

Unit 2

1 Find five sentences.

Begin with the words in circles. Go → ↓ ↑ or ←

is	Is	that	photo	(My)	camera
(These)	Harry's	your	dog?	room	big
are	the	(My) ↓	heavy	isn't	very
mouse	photos	sister →	is →	very ↓	your
tiger	from	(Cosmo)	and	tall	cats
picnic	the	are	Bella	are	Harry's

2 Unjumble this sentence.

Clue: The sentence is in Unit 2.

> photos   from   the
>
> party   Sarah's   birthday
>
> are   These

....

3 Write a jumbled sentence for your partner. Use a sentence from Unit 2.

....

36

Unit 3

1 Find and write.

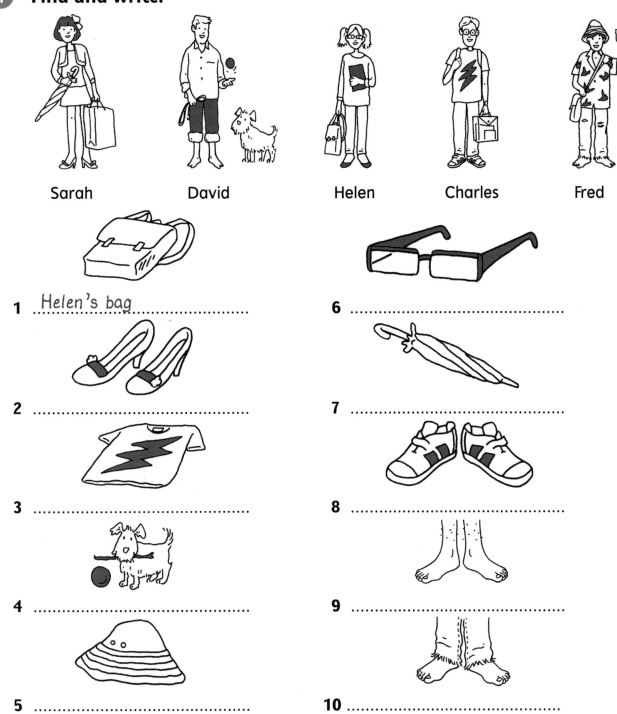

Sarah   David   Helen   Charles   Fred

1 Helen's bag
2 ....
3 ....
4 ....
5 ....
6 ....
7 ....
8 ....
9 ....
10 ....

2 Match.

1 There's a swimming pool — on the roof of — is very funny.
2 The end of — the capital of — that house.
3 There are two birds — at the back of — this T-shirt.
4 Madrid is — on the top of — our school.
5 I don't like — this film — that mountain.
6 There's a little house — the colour of — Spain.

Grammar Time 3

Unit 4

A

1 **Ask and answer to complete the table. Write [✓] or [✗].**

B: Have Fred's mum and dad got a car?
A: Yes, they have.

B: Has Helen got a cat?
A: No, she hasn't.

	a dog	a cat	a computer	a car
Fred	✗			✗
Helen		✗	✓	
Helen's mum and dad	✓		✗	
Fred's mum and dad		✗		✓

2 **Write sentences.**

1 Fred's mum and dad / car — Fred's mum and dad have got a car.
2 Helen / dog
3 Fred's mum and dad / computer
4 Fred / computer
5 Helen's mum and dad / a car

B

1 **Ask and answer to complete the table. Write [✓] or [✗].**

A: Have Helen's mum and dad got a cat?
B: Yes, they have.

A: Has Fred got a computer?
B: No, he hasn't.

	a dog	a cat	a computer	a car
Fred		✓	✗	
Helen	✓			✗
Helen's mum and dad		✓		✗
Fred's mum and dad	✗		✓	

2 **Write sentences.**

1 Helen's mum and dad / cat — Helen's mum and dad have got a cat.
2 Helen / cat
3 Fred's mum and dad / car
4 Fred / dog
5 Helen's mum and dad / computer

Unit 5

1 Read and draw.

1 There's a snake under the box.

2 There's a tree next to the house.

3 There's a spider between the book and the box.

4 There's a mouse in front of the box. There's a cat behind the box.

5 There are two mice on the box. There's a ball near the box.

6 There's a tree opposite the house.

2 Read the clues and complete the grid. Find the mystery word.

Clues:
1 *TeenLink* is the school _____ .
2 'Why aren't you at school?' – '_____ it's Saturday.'
3 On Beth's desk, there's a _____ next to the laptop. (look at page 25)
4 A _____ is a small computer.
5 My dad is __ __ work today.
6 I clean my teeth with my _____ .

The mystery word is _____ .

Grammar Time 3

Unit 6

1 Make and say sentences. Work in pairs and take turns.

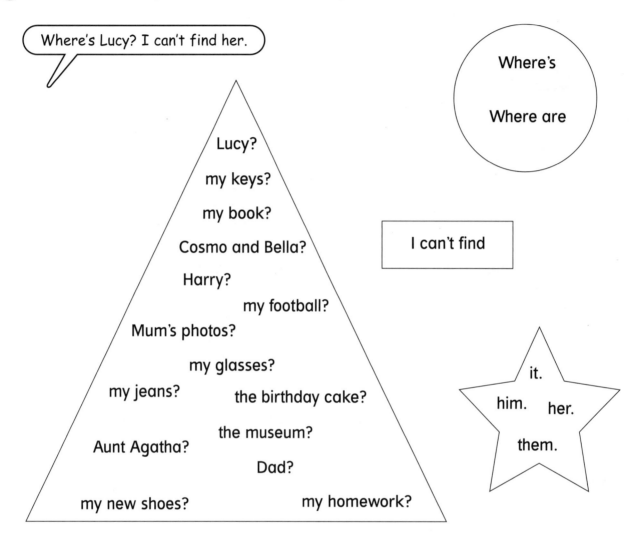

2 Write sentences from Exercise 1.

1. Where's Lucy? I can't find her.
2. ....
3. ....
4. ....
5. ....
6. ....
7. ....
8. ....
9. ....
10. ....

Photocopiable Activity Sheet

Unit 7

A

1 Ask and answer to complete the text.

Use these words

What time does …?   Where does …?
What does …?   How often does …?

B: What time does David get up?   A: He gets up at seven o'clock.

On Saturdays –
David gets up at seven o'clock.
He does his homework in the morning.
He has pizza and salad for lunch.
He goes to the sports centre in the afternoon.
He visit his best friend in the evening.
He brushes his teeth three times a day.

On Saturdays –
Fred gets up at ....
He .... in the morning.
He has .... for lunch.
He goes to .... in the afternoon.
He .... in the evening.
He brushes his teeth ....

B

1 Ask and answer with a friend.

Use these words

What time does …?   Where does …?
What does …?   How often does …?

A: What time does Fred get up?   B: He gets up at ten o'clock.

On Saturdays –
Fred gets up at ten o'clock.
He watches TV in the morning.
He has three burgers for lunch.
He goes to the beach in the afternoon.
He plays computer games in the evening.
He brushes his teeth twice a day.

On Saturdays –
David gets up at ....
He .... in the morning.
He has .... for lunch.
He goes to .... in the afternoon.
He .... in the evening.
He brushes his teeth ....

Grammar Time 3

Unit 8

1 **Choose the correct word.**

TeenLink

My Sundays
I **¹ every day / usually** *get up at eleven o'clock on Sundays.*
I **² always / never** *get up early. I have breakfast and then I watch TV.*
I **³ often / once** *phone my friends, but they usually* **⁴ goes / go** *to the park on Sundays. Sometimes I* **⁵ read / watch** *magazines. We always have lunch* **⁶ at / in** *one o'clock. I usually eat a pizza.* **⁷ Always / Sometimes** *I eat two pizzas.* **⁸ In / At** *the afternoon I often take a nap.*

2 **Find and underline one answer which is not possible.**

1   A: How often do you go to the supermarket?
    B: I go there once a week. / I never go to the supermarket. / <u>Yes, I do.</u>

2   A: Do you often go to the cinema?
    B: At seven o'clock. / No, I don't. / Yes, I do. There's a cinema near my house.

3   A: Are you usually late for school?
    B: No, I'm not. / Yes, sometimes. / No, I don't.

4   A: What do you do at the weekends?
    B: We sometimes visit my aunt and uncle. / No, I don't. I never go to the cinema. / I usually go shopping with my brother.

5   A: Do you sometimes get up late?
    B: Yes, I do. I always get up at seven o'clock. / No, I don't. I always get up early. / Yes, I do.

6   A: Where do you usually go on holiday?
    B: We sometimes go to the mountains. / I don't usually go on holiday. / No, I don't.

Unit 9

1 Find six sentences.

Begin with the words in circles. Go → ↓ ↑ or ←

at →	the →	moment.	breakfast	my	always
↑					
English ←	studying	(I)	play	football	every
	↑				
(We)	(I'm)	is	doing	his	day.
always	(My)	brother	are	homework	right
have	(Our)	teacher	plays	tennis	now.
lunch	at	week.	a	once	twice
o'clock.	twelve	with	staying	you	not
week.	this	us	is	cousin	(My)

2 Unjumble this sentence.

Clue: The sentence is in Unit 9.

```
   your                              a
              always
   have                         party
              birthday
          We             on
```

....

3 Write a jumbled sentence for your friend. Use a sentence from Unit 9.

....

Grammar Time 3

Unit 10

1 Choose the true answer.

1 Do you like football?   Yes, I do. / No, I don't.
2 Do you like dancing?   Yes, I do. / No, I don't.
3 Are you good at drawing?   Yes, I am. / No, I'm not.
4 Are you crazy about computers?   Yes, I am. / No, I'm not.
5 Do you like shopping?   Yes, I do. / No, I don't.
6 Do you want to be a teacher?   Yes, I do. / No, I don't.

2 Ask two friends. Write [✓] or [✗].

All about you!

name: ....   name: ....

Do you like football?

Do you like dancing?

Are you good at drawing?

Are you crazy about computers?

Do you like shopping?

Do you want to be a teacher?

3 Write about your friends.

Sylvia likes dancing.
Marco is crazy about computers.
....
....
....
....
....

Unit 11

1 **Look and correct the sentences.**

1 There isn't any fruit in the bowl. [✗]
   There's some fruit in the bowl.

2 There are some sandwiches in the fridge. [✗]
   ....

3 There isn't any milk in the fridge. [✗]
   ....

4 There aren't any bananas in the bowl. [✗]
   ....

5 There are two cakes in the fridge. [✗]
   ....

6 There are some eggs in the fridge. [✗]
   ....

7 There's one orange in the bowl. [✗]
   ....

2 **Write the words under the correct heading. Then find them in the word square.**

banana   ~~biscuit~~   bottle   cheese   chocolate   coffee   egg   pancake
popcorn   sandwich   water   yoghurt

Countable nouns		Uncountable nouns
biscuit	N A H P E L E C T E G G	....
	P A N C A K E H P F N A	
....	C A L H E L T E O S C W	....
	O O N O H T E E P B M A	
....	F Y T C R (B I S C U I T)	....
	F H G O U R O E O B Y E	
....	E T G L N I N N R K O R	....
	E N T A X I R B N N G O	
....	B O T T L E K C O T H S	....
	A H P E A L C L L E U W	
	O S A N D W I C H C R M	
	A B E B A N A N A Q T M	

Grammar Time 3

Unit 12

1 Match and make sentences.

1 There are — a lot of children — near my school.
2 There isn't — much water — on the beach today.
3 There are — much cheese — in my class.
4 There aren't — a lot of people — in that packet.
5 There aren't — many shops — in that bottle.
6 There isn't — many biscuits — on this pizza.

2 Read and write the children's names.

Ben   Bill   ~~Emma~~   Jenny   Nick   Nina   Peter   Sally

- There are three books on Jenny's desk.
- Nina and Bill have got bags.
- Nick is between Ben and Nina.
- Ben is writing in his notebook.
- There's a mouse under Peter's desk.
- Sally is next to Jenny.

1 .... 2 .... 3 .... 4 .... 5 .... 6 .... 7 Emma 8 ....

Unit 13

1 Read and match.

Where were they yesterday afternoon?

- David was at the cinema.
- Sarah wasn't at the cinema.
- One boy was at home.
- David was with Charles's sister.
- One girl was at the hairdresser's.
- Charles is Helen's brother.
- Fred wasn't at home.
- Helen was with David.

| Sarah | David | Helen | Charles | Fred |

at the cinema   at home   at Charles's house   at the hairdresser's   at the cinema

2 Are these sentences true (T) or false (F)?

1 Sarah was at home yesterday afternoon. …F…
2 Helen wasn't with her brother. ………
3 David wasn't at home. ………
4 Fred was with David. ………
5 Helen was at the hairdresser's. ………
6 Fred was at Charles's house. ………

3 Write answers.

1 Where were Charles and Fred? …They……………………
2 Who was at home? ………………………
3 Who was with Helen? ………………………
4 Where was Sarah? ………………………
5 Was Helen at the hairdresser's? ………………………

Unit 14

1 **Find six sentences in the Past simple**

Begin with the words in circles. Go → ↓ ↑ or ←

saw	(My)↓	word	(We)	didn't	go
ate ←	dog	(I)	saw	a	to
my↓	eat	player.	football	famous	the
birthday↓	his	homework	wrote	(Lucy)	supermarket
cake!	finished	an	a	is	yesterday.
(My)	(He)	hour	letter	to	her
dad	bought	ago.	my	mum.	friend
buy	some	flowers	for	Japan.	in

2 **Unjumble this sentence.**

Clue: The sentence is in Unit 14.

the   food!   Cosmo   chewed   box   the   ate   cat   and

....

3 **Write a jumbled sentence for your friend. Use a sentence from Unit 14.**

....

Unit 15

A

1 Complete the questions.

> country   favourite   food   speak   ~~subject~~   want

1 What's Helen's favourite ....*subject*....?
2 What's her .... sport?
3 What's her favourite ....?
4 What language can she ....?
5 Which .... would she like to visit?
6 What does she .... to be when she grows up?

2 Ask Student B questions from Exercise 1 to complete the information about Helen.

Helen's favourite subject is ....
Her favourite sport is ....
Her favourite food is ....
She can speak ....
She would like to visit ....
She wants to be ....

3 Now answer Student B's questions about David.

David's favourite subject is History.
His favourite sport is football.
His favourite food is ice cream.
He can speak French.
He would like to visit the USA.
He wants to be a doctor.

B

1 Complete the questions.

> country   favourite   food   speak   ~~subject~~   want

1 What's David's favourite ....*subject*....?
2 What's his .... sport?
3 What's his favourite ....?
4 What language can he ....?
5 Which .... would he like to visit?
6 What does he .... to be when he grows up?

2 Answer Student A's questions about Helen.

Helen's favourite subject is English.
Her favourite sport is swimming.
Her favourite food is chicken.
She can speak Spanish.
She would like to visit Australia.
She wants to be a teacher.

3 Ask Student A questions from Exercise 1 to complete the information about David.

David's favourite subject is ....
His favourite sport is ....
His favourite food is ....
He can speak ....
He would like to visit ....
He wants to be ....

Grammar Time 3

Unit 16

1 Look at the pictures and complete the grid. Find the mystery animal.

1. (cat) 2. (shark) 3. (horse)
4. (parrot) 5. (snake) 6. (hamster)
7. (iguana) 8. (goldfish) 9. (alsatian)

The mystery animal is _____ .

2 Match.

1 Sharks are more   tarantulas.
2 Hamsters are prettier than   intelligent than snakes.
3 Dogs are more expensive   better pets than iguanas.
4 Parrots are more   dangerous than dolphins.
5 Alsatians are   intelligent animals in the world.
6 People are the most   stronger than poodles.
7 Dogs are   than hamsters.

50

Unit 17

1) Find and underline one answer which is not possible.

1 I dance very ...
   <u>bad</u>   well   badly
2 English people sometimes speak very ...
   quick   quickly   fast
3 My best friend is often very ...
   funny   quietly   lazy
4 Please finish this exercise ...
   untidy   neatly   quietly
5 My dad works very ...
   good   hard   fast
6 My mum always drives ...
   safely   carefully   safe
7 Horses are ... animals.
   quickly   beautiful   nice
8 Peter did his English homework very ...
   carefully   fast   careful

2) Play a guessing game.

Student A: Think of a famous person. Don't tell Student B. Write the first letters of the person's name on a piece of paper.

Student B: Guess your friend's person. Ask these questions:

	it	a / an man? / woman?
Is	he	a / an football player? / actor? / politician?
	she	young? / old? / tall? / short? / fat? / thin?
	from	Spain? / Italy? / France? / the USA?

Grammar Time 3

Unit 18

1 **Choose the correct word.**

are   going   is   rain   ~~take~~   wash

1 She is going to ...*take*... a photo.

2 He .... going to open the window.

3 They .... going to fall in the water.

4 He is .... to paint the door.

5 They are going to .... the car.

6 It is going to ....

2 **Now draw the pictures.**

Unit 19

1 Match the sentences with the pictures.

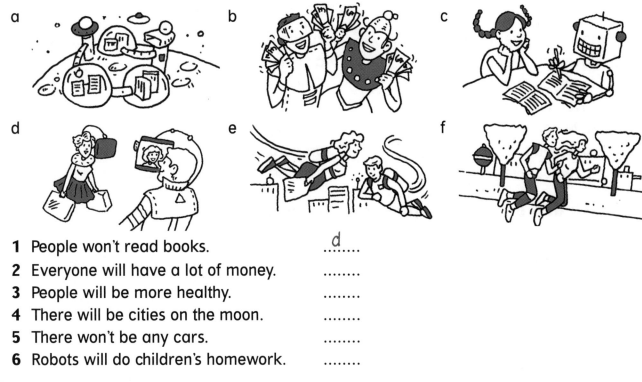

1 People won't read books. ....d....
2 Everyone will have a lot of money. ....
3 People will be more healthy. ....
4 There will be cities on the moon. ....
5 There won't be any cars. ....
6 Robots will do children's homework. ....

2 Ask your friends. Write [✓] or [✗].

A: Do you think people won't read books?
B: Yes, I do. / No, I don't.

In the future Do you think ...	name	name	name ....
1 people won't read books?	☐	☐	☐
2 everyone will have a lot of money?	☐	☐	☐
3 people will be more healthy?	☐	☐	☐
4 there will be cities on the moon?	☐	☐	☐
5 there won't be any cars?	☐	☐	☐
6 robots will do children's homework?	☐	☐	☐

3 Write about your friends.

Sylvia thinks people won't read books.
Marco doesn't think everyone will have a lot of money.
....
....
....
....

Grammar Time 3

Units 20 & 21

1 Match. Then answer the questions for you. Write [✓] or [X].

			You	Your friend
1	Have you ever fallen off	London?	....	....
2	Have you ever eaten	a snake?	....	....
3	Have you ever been to	Chinese food?	....	....
4	Have you ever swum in	your bike?	....	....
5	Have you ever broken	the sea?	....	....
6	Have you ever seen	an aeroplane?	....	....
7	Have you ever been in	your arm?	....	....

2 Ask and answer the questions in Exercise 1.

A: Have you ever fallen off your bike?

B: Yes, I have. / No, I haven't.

3 Write about you and your friend.

I have fallen off my bike.
Enrique has never fallen off his bike.
....
....
....
....
....
....
....
....
....
....

Photocopiable Activity Sheet

Unit 22

1 **Make and say rules for the class. Work in pairs and take turns.**

We mustn't be late.

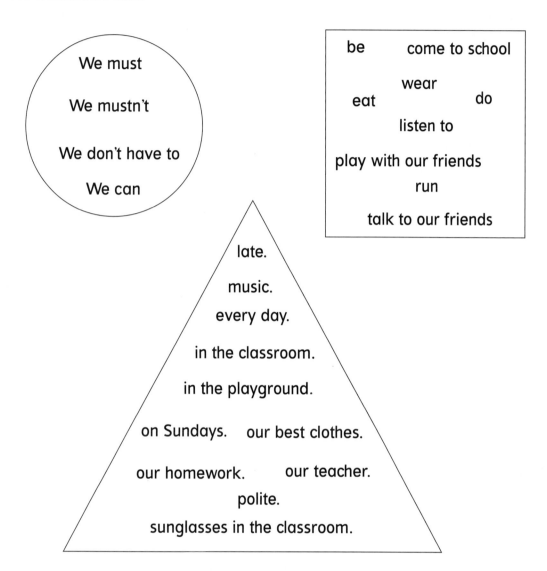

2 **Write your rules from Exercise 1.**

1 We mustn't be late. ....
2 ....
3 ....
4 ....
5 ....
6 ....
7 ....
8 ....
9 ....
10 ....

Grammar Time 3

Unit 23

1 Find and underline one answer which is not possible.

1 A: I'm hungry.
  B: Let's go to McDonald's. ✏ <u>That's a good idea.</u> ✏ Shall I make some sandwiches?
2 A: I want to get up early tomorrow.
  B: Yes, you're right. ✏ You mustn't stay up late tonight. ✏ You should go to bed early.
3 A: I've got a headache.
  B: You shouldn't play on the computer all day. ✏ Really? Shall I get you some aspirin?
    ✏ I'll show you.
4 A: Would you like to play a computer game?
  B: No. I've got a headache. ✏ Yes, OK. ✏ Shall I give it to you?
5 A: I can't do this exercise!
  B: You should see a dentist. ✏ I'll help you. ✏ You should ask your teacher about it.
6 A: Shall we go to the beach?
  B: Good idea! ✏ Thanks. ✏ Yes. Let's invite Ben, too.

2 Read the clues and complete the grid. Find the mystery word.

1 This exercise is very _____. I can't do it.
2 A: I've got a terrible _____.
  B: You should see a dentist.
3 We _____n't eat in the classroom.
4 Mum, your mobile _____ is ringing!
5 A: I'm hungry.
  B: OK. Let's make some _____.
6 A: This box is heavy.
  B: Shall I _____ it for you?
7 A: I've got a _____.
  B: I'll get you some aspirin.'
8 I'm _____ this morning. I watched TV until 12.30 last night.

1												
2												
3												
4												
5												
6												
7												
8												

The mystery word is _____.

Unit 24

1 Read and match.

What were they doing at six o'clock yesterday evening?

- One girl was playing volleyball.
- Helen's dad was washing his car.
- Fred's best friend was waiting for a bus.
- One boy was making a model aeroplane.
- Helen was helping her dad.
- David is Fred's best friend.
- Fred was sleeping.
- Charles wasn't waiting for a bus.

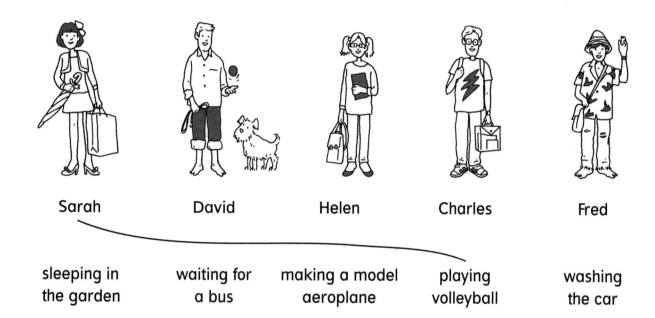

| Sarah | David | Helen | Charles | Fred |

| sleeping in the garden | waiting for a bus | making a model aeroplane | playing volleyball | washing the car |

2 Are these sentences true (T) or false (F)?

1 Fred was with David.   _F_
2 Sarah was doing her homework.   ....
3 Fred wasn't doing his homework. ....
4 David was waiting for a bus.   ....
5 Helen was with her dad.   ....
6 Charles was helping Helen.   ....

3 Write answers.

1 What were Helen and her dad doing?   _They_ ....
2 Who was playing volleyball?   ....
3 Was Charles making a model aeroplane? ....
4 Was David playing volleyball?   ....
5 What was Fred doing?   ....

Grammar Time 3

Unit 25

1 Make and say questions. Work in pairs and take turns.

What's your favourite colour?

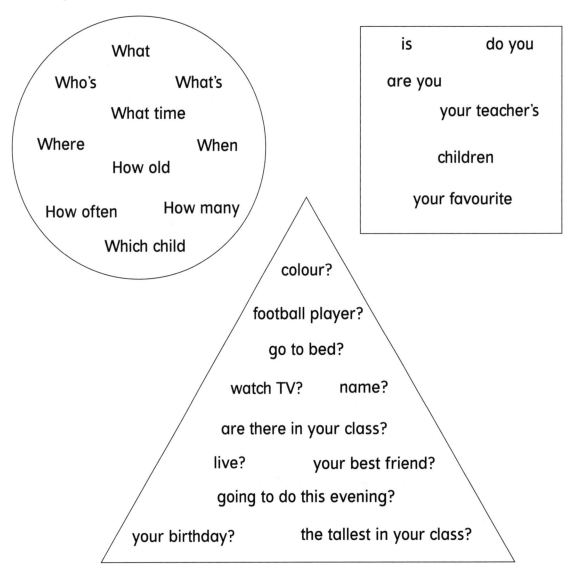

2 Write the questions from Exercise 1. Then answer the questions.

1 What's your favourite colour?   My favourite colour is ....
2 ....
3 ....
4 ....
5 ....
6 ....
7 ....
8 ....
9 ....
10 ....

58

Grammar Time 3 — Photocopiable quiz sheets

Quiz 1

Name: .... Date: .... Total: ..../20

A Tick (✓) the correct sentence in each pair.

1 a Cosmo and Bella is Harry's cats. ✗
  b Cosmo and Bella are Harry's cats. ✓
2 a This is Sam. He's my brother. ☐
  b This is Sam. She's my brother. ☐
3 a A: What's your name?
     B: San Francisco. ☐
  b A: Where are you from?
     B: San Francisco. ☐
4 a Who in the school basketball team. ☐
  b We're in the school basketball team. ☐
5 a A: What's your favourite colour?
     B: Green. ☐
  b A: What's your favourite subject?
     B: Green. ☐
6 a How old are you? ☐
  b How old you are? ☐

Score: ..../5

B Find the extra, incorrect word in each sentence.

1 ~~How~~ Is Cosmo a cat?
2 I'm not old very hungry.
3 Harry is and Peter are neighbours.
4 How tall your are you?
5 My birthday best party is tomorrow.
6 What is your teacher's friend name?

Score: ..../5

C Write the extra words from Exercise B. Then answer the question.

How ....? ....

Score: ..../1

D Tick (✓) the correct answer.

1 What's that bird in the tree?
   a Wow! This is a parrot. ☐
   b Wow! It's a parrot. ☐
2 Are these your photos?
   a Yes, it is. ☐
   b No, they aren't. ☐
3 Who are those people over there?
   a That's Peter and Harry. ☐
   b This is Peter and Harry. ☐
4 Is this your umbrella?
   a No, they aren't. ☐
   b Yes, it is. ☐
5 What are all these things?
   a They're my little brother's toys. ☐
   b It's my little brother's toy. ☐
6 Is that your mum's car?
   a No, she isn't. ☐
   b Yes, it is. ☐

Score: ..../5

E Choose and circle.

1 This is … old photo.   a   (an)   the
2 Are … kangaroos from Australia?   a   an   the
3 My friend and I are in … same class.   a   an   the
4 A Porsche is … expensive car.   a   an   the
5 Mr Smith is … new head teacher at our school.   a   an   the

Score: ..../4

Grammar Time 3

Quiz 2

Name: .... Date: .... Total: ..../20

A Circle the correct answer.

1 Is that your **friends / friend / (friend's)** house?
2 Those **boys' / boys / boy's** bikes are exactly the same.
3 Sam's **shoe's / shoes' / shoes** are in his bedroom.
4 What's your **sisters / sister's / sisters'** name?
5 What are your **brother's / brothers / brothers'** names?
6 *Toy Story* is a **children's / childrens / childrens'** film.

Score: ..../5

B Choose and write the correct word. There is one extra word.

back   capital   end   name   roof   top   ~~walls~~

1 I like the pictures on the ...*walls*... of our classroom.
2 Do you know the .... of this street?
3 Please read the words at the .... of the page.
4 The .... of this film is very funny.
5 The .... of Spain is Madrid.
6 There's a sports centre at the .... of our school.

Score: ..../5

C Write one word.

1 I ...*have*... got a new bike.
2 Have all your friends .... computers?
3 My school .... got a swimming pool.
4 **A:** Has your brother got blond hair?
   B: .... he hasn't.
5 **A:** Have your grandparents got a dog?
   B: No. ....'ve got a cat.
6 We .... got a TV in our classroom.

Score: ..../5

D Circle the correct answer.

1 **A:** Whose book is this?
   B: It's **(mine) / my**.
2 Lucy's my best friend and I'm **hers / her**.
3 **A:** Dad's car is the red car.
   B: OK. **Who / Whose** is the green car?
4 Hi! My name's Simon. What's **your / yours**?
5 **A:** Are they Harry's cats?
   B: Yes. They're **his / hers**.
6 **A:** Is Bob your parents' dog?
   B: No. Bob is my dog. **Hers / Theirs** is Sam.

Score: ..../5

Grammar Time 3 Photocopiable quiz sheets

Quiz 3

Name: .... Date: .... Total: ..../20

A Tick (✓) the correct sentence in each pair.

1 a There isn't a swimming pool in our town. ✓
  b There aren't a swimming pool in our town. ✗
2 a A: Are there trees near your school?
    B: No, there aren't. ☐
  b A: Are there trees near your school?
    B: No, there isn't. ☐
3 a There are three books on my desk. ☐
  b There is three books on my desk. ☐
4 a There are a spider in the bath. ☐
  b There's a spider in the bath. ☐
5 a There are fifteen girl in our class. ☐
  b There are fifteen girls in our class. ☐

Score: ..../4

B Read and draw.

1 There's a man in the car.
2 There's a dog in the car. It's next to the man.
3 There's a tree behind the car.
4 There's a ball under the car.
5 There's a river in front of the car.
6 The car is between two sheep.

Score: ..../5

C Read the sentences about your school. Tick (✓) the true sentences. Change the incorrect sentences.

1 Our school is near the road. ✓
2 Our school is ~~very small~~ ..big............
3 There's a supermarket near our school.
4 There's a cinema opposite our school.
5 There's a café next to our school.
6 Today there are three cars in front of our school.

Score: ..../4

D Find the extra, incorrect word in each sentence.

1 Are ~~Is~~ there shops in your street?
2 There's a bus in front of our school.
3 My house has a four windows.
4 There are two cinema in my town.
5 My school in is opposite a nice park.
6 Look out! There's a chimp your behind you.
7 There are two books on Lucy's town desk.

Score: ..../6

E Write the extra words from Exercise D. Then answer the question.

..Is............. .... ? ....

Score: ..../1

Photocopiable © Pearson Education Limited 2008 61

Grammar Time 3

Quiz 4

Name: .... Date: .... Total: ..../20

A Circle the correct word.

1 Where are my keys? I can't find **them** / **they**.
2 Where's Dad? I can't see **he** / **him**.
3 There's Dad. DAD! … He can't hear **we** / **us**.
4 I'm OK. Don't worry about **me** / **my**.
5 Can **us** / **we** play in the garden, Mum?
6 Mrs Jones is our teacher. We like **her** / **him**.

Score: ..../5

B Write one word.

A: What ¹ _time_ do you get up?
B: At seven o'clock.
A: ² .... do you have for breakfast?
B: Cornflakes, milk and orange juice.
A: Do ³ .... walk to school?
B: No. I go by bus.
A: Do your friends go on the same bus?
B: Yes, ⁴ .... do.

A: Do you have an English lesson every day?
B: No. We have English lessons three ⁵ .... a week.
A: Do you go to school ⁶ .... Sundays?
B: No, I don't.

Score: ..../5

C Tick (✓) the correct answer.

1 What do you usually do on Sundays?
   a Yes, I do. ✗
   b I do my homework and I play computer games. ✓
2 Do you often go to the zoo?
   a Yes, it does. ☐
   b No, we don't. ☐
3 What time do your lessons start?
   a At nine o'clock. ☐
   b Yes, they do. ☐
4 Do your friends usually wear jeans?
   a Yes, they do. ☐
   b Yes, she does. ☐
5 Does it often rain in the winter?
   a Yes, it is. ☐
   b Yes, it does. ☐
6 How do you spend the holidays?
   a I often visit my grandparents. ☐
   b No, I don't. ☐

Score: ..../5

D Put the words in the correct order.

1 in often my friends meet I the park   _I sometimes meet my friends in the park._
2 I the morning watch TV in sometimes   ....
3 three times football play a week I   ....
4 on Sundays always go to bed I early   ....
5 My mum Fridays goes shopping usually on   ....
6 never cinema the We at weekend the go to ....

Score: ..../5

Grammar Time 3 — Photocopiable quiz sheets

Quiz 5

Name: .... Date: .... Total: ..../20

A Circle the correct answer.

Hi!
We're on holiday. We [1] **stay / (are staying) / is staying** in a house near the sea.
[2] **It's / He's / It** raining today!
I'm [3] **write / writing / is writing** e-mails. My brother and sister are [4] **watch / they / watching** TV. Mum and Dad [5] **are / is / they** tidying the kitchen. Our dog Sid [6] **is / he's / he** sleeping.
It's cold. I [7] **wear / am wearing / are wearing** three T-shirts!
What are [8] **you do / doing / you doing** today?

Score: ..../7

B Complete with the present simple or present continuous.

1 *I'm staying* at my friend's house this weekend. (stay)
2 My sister *washes* her hair every morning. (wash)
3 Dad .... the car right now. (wash)
4 We .... to the cinema on Sundays. (not go)
5 It .... at the moment. (not rain)

Score: ..../3

C Tick (✓) the correct sentence in each pair.

1 **a** I don't want to go to the cinema. ✓
   b I don't want go to the cinema. ✗
2 **a** My brother hates tidy his room. ☐
   b My brother hates tidying his room. ☐
3 **a** Do you want to being a footballer? ☐
   b Do you want to be a footballer? ☐
4 **a** Our cat likes watching birds. ☐
   b Our cat likes watch birds. ☐
5 **a** My dad is very good at make pizzas. ☐
   b My dad is very good at making pizzas. ☐
6 **a** I'd like meeting Jennifer Lopez. ☐
   b I'd like to meet Jennifer Lopez. ☐

Score: ..../5

D Choose and write.

good for you.
with playing computer games.
going to restaurants.
~~is very good exercise.~~
in visiting museums.
visit France.

1 Swimming *is very good exercise.*
2 I'd love to ....
3 My mum and dad enjoy ....
4 Going to bed late every night isn't ....
5 Mum is very interested ....
6 Let's play football. I'm bored ....

Score: ..../5

Grammar Time 3

Quiz 6

Name: .... Date: .... Total: ..../20

A **Choose and circle.**

1 There are … apples in the bowl.	(no)	a lot	any
2 There isn't … of water in that bottle.	a lot	some	no
3 There is … cheese in the fridge.	any	some	many
4 I can't see … cats in the garden.	a lot	any	much
5 Is there … yoghurt in the fridge?	a lot	many	any
6 There are … shops in our road.	any	no	much

Score: ..../5

B **Circle the correct word.**

1 The box is empty. There's **anything /(nothing)** in it.
2 **A:** Can you hear that music?
  B: No. I can't hear **anything / nothing**.
3 Listen! There's **somewhere / someone** in the kitchen.
4 I can't find my book **anyone / anywhere**.
5 Come here, Joe. Mum wants to tell you **something / someone**.
6 It's raining. There's **no one / nothing** in the park.

Score: ..../5

C **Find the extra, incorrect word in each sentence.**

1 ~~How~~ Harry likes healthy food.
2 I haven't got much many money.
3 There aren't many people eggs in the fridge.
4 There live are a lot of shops in this town.
5 I drink two litres of water in every day.
6 How many biscuits do your you want?
7 There are twenty students house in our class.

Score: ..../6

D **Write the extra words from Exercise C. Then answer the question.**

1 How .... ?
....

Score: ..../1

E **Circle the correct word.**

1 a loaf of   cola   (bread)   chocolate   3 a slice of   soup   pizza   milk
2 a bottle of   bread   pizza   water   4 a can of   flour   bread   cola

Score: ..../3

Grammar Time 3 — Photocopiable quiz sheets

Quiz 7

Name: .... Date: .... Total: ..../20

A Write *was* or *were*.

1 Where ...*were*........ you yesterday morning?
2 .... you sister at home yesterday?
3 I .... n't at school yesterday.
4 We .... at the cinema last night.
5 There .... a lot of people at the cinema.

Score: ..../4

B Find the extra, incorrect word in each sentence.

1 Was ~~Were~~ Lucy at the cinema last night?
2 Were there you a lot of people at the cinema?
3 I was with my friends at yesterday afternoon.
4 We were at the sports school centre.
5 My family and I were in Spain yesterday three weeks ago.
6 Where were you afternoon last night?

Score: ..../5

C Write the extra words from Exercise B. Then answer the question.

Were .... ?
....

Score: ..../1

D Complete with the past simple.

A: What did you do yesterday? ¹ ...*Did you go*......... (you / go) to the sports centre?
B: No, I ² .... Ben and I ³ .... (stay) at home and we
   ⁴ .... (make) a present for our dad. It's his birthday on Saturday.
A: What ⁵ .... (you / make)?
B: We ⁶ .... (paint) his favourite chair. What did you do?
A: I ⁷ .... (go) to the shopping centre with my friend, Laura.
   We ⁸ .... (buy) some CDs.
B: ⁹ .... (you / walk) to the shopping centre?
A: No, we ¹⁰ .... We ¹¹ .... (take) the bus.

Score: ..../10

Quiz 8

Name: .... Date: .... Total: ..../20

A Choose and circle.

1 I never watch TV in … morning.   a   (the)   –
2 Oranges cost £1… kilo.   a   –   the
3 My brother can play … violin.   –   an   the
4 A: What are you doing?
   B: I'm writing … email.   the   an   a
5 My friend Sam is from … USA.   –   the   a
6 A: Do you like … Maths?
   B: Yes, I do.   –   a   the

Score: ..../5

B Tick (✓) the correct sentence in each pair.

1 a I'm tallest than Emma.
   b I'm taller than Emma.
2 a Dogs are more intelligent than cats.
   b Dogs are most intelligent than cats.
3 a My cat is the most beautiful cat in the world.
   b My cat is the more beautiful cat in the world.
4 a Emma is the most old girl in our class. ✗
   b Emma is the oldest girl in our class. ✓
5 a A: Is your sister's room bigger than yours?
   b A: Is your sister's room more big than yours?
6 a B: Yes, it is. But my room is nicer.
   b B: Yes, it is. But my room is nicest than hers.

Score: ..../5

C Complete with the correct form of the comparative or the superlative.

1 Parrots are ...*more interesting than*... (interesting) goldfish.
2 Dogs are .... (popular) pet in the world.
3 Sharks are .... (big) than dolphins.
4 Alsatians are .... (strong) than poodles.
5 Dogs are .... (good) pets than hamsters.
6 Snakes are .... (bad) pet: they sleep all the time.

Score: ..../5

D Choose and complete.

> badly ~~clearly~~ easy easily fast polite

1 My brother doesn't write very ...*clearly*....
2 Sam has got a lot of friends. He makes friends ....
3 My dad is a .... swimmer.
4 I dance very .... – I hate dancing!
5 My friend Sam is always ....
6 This homework isn't difficult, it's very ....

Score: ..../5

Quiz 9

Name: .... Date: .... Total: ..../20

A Write one word.

1 We're *going* to go out for a walk.
2 A: Are you going to stay in this evening?
   B: No, I'm ....
3 Mum and Dad .... going to come to the school play.
4 I want to stay in today. I'm .... going to visit my friends.
5 Beth .... going to have lunch with Angela on Saturday.
6 A: Are you and your friends going to play football tomorrow?
   B: Yes, we ....

Score: ..../5

B Choose and write.

aren't going to have a party on their birthday.   go out for a walk.
do at the weekend?   a present for my mum.
going to rain.   to go to the hairdresser's?
going to visit her uncle on Saturday?

1 I'm going to buy *a present for my mum.*
2 What are you going to ....
3 Is Beth ....
4 On no! It's ....
5 What time are you going ....
6 Sam and Ben ....

Score: ..../5

C Put the words in the correct order.

1 will our team hope I win   *I hope our team will win.*
2 you'll I a famous artist be think ....
3 hope play the piano won't I Aunt Agatha ....
4 busy today won't It on the beach be ....
5 you What school? after will do ....
6 here a hotel years' in There ten be will time ....

Score: ..../5

D Choose and complete.

be   come   cook   *go*   have   work

I want to be a famous cook. After school, I'll ¹ *go* to France and I'll ² .... in a restaurant. In ten years time I'll ³ .... a restaurant. I won't ⁴ .... fast food. I will make fantastic burgers with lovely salad. Lots of people will ⁵ .... to my restaurant. Its name will ⁶ .... *Beautiful Burgers.*

Score: ..../5

Grammar Time 3

Quiz 10

Name: .... Date: .... Total: ..../20

A Nina and her brother Ben are very busy today. Look at their TO DO lists and answer the questions. Use short answers.

TO DO	Ben
1 buy a present for Mum	✔
2 do my homework	✔
3 write a letter to Aunt Liz	✗
4 clean my football boots	✔
5 read my new book	✗
6 wash Dad's car	✔

TO DO	Nina
1 tidy my room	✗
2 finish my History project	✗
3 take a photo of Jim (our new cat)	✔
4 send the photo to Izumi	✗
5 put Jim's basket in my room	✔
6 buy a present for Mum	✔

1 Has Ben cleaned his football boots? *Yes, he has.*
2 Has Nina taken a photo of her cat? ....
3 Has she sent it to Izumi? ....
4 Have Ben and Nina bought a present for their mum? ....
5 Has Ben written a letter to Aunt Liz? ....
6 Has Nina finished her History project? ....

Score: ..../5

B Look at Exercise A. Write one word.

1 Ben has *done* his homework.
2 Nina hasn't .... her room.
3 Ben has .... his dad's car.
4 Ben and Nina .... bought a present for their mum.
5 Ben hasn't .... his new book.
6 Nina has .... Jim's basket in her room.

Score: ..../5

C Put the words in the correct order.

1 you to Australia? Have been ever *Have you ever been to Australia?*
2 a bus? your mum Has driven ever ....
3 slept Harry in a tent? Has ever ....
4 you seen Have a dolphin? ever ....
5 your dad ever a pizza? Has made ....
6 Have tried your friends ever Chinese food? ....

Score: ..../5

D Choose the correct word.

1 Our teacher is happy. She's **ever / just / yet** come back from holiday.
2 I haven't told Ben about the party **already / never / yet**.
3 I've **ever / yet / never** been to London.
4 My brother has **ever / just / yet** broken Mum's favourite vase.
5 I've **already / yet / ever** done my homework.
6 My grandfather has **ever / never / yet** watched a DVD.

Score: ..../5

Quiz 11

Name: .... Date: .... Total: ..../20

A Write sentences with *can*, *can't*, *could* or *couldn't*. Use the verbs in brackets.

1 Sorry, you *can't use* (not / use) my computer. I need it for my homework.
2 I *could ride* (ride) a bike when I was five years old.
3 I .... (not / find) my dictionary. Perhaps it's at school.
4 My teacher .... (not / drive).
5 My dad is very good at languages. He .... (speak) English, French and Chinese!
6 .... (I / borrow) your calculator, please?
7 My brother .... (swim) now, but he .... (not / swim) last year.

Score: ..../6

B Choose the correct word.

1 Dad loves the weekend. He **must / has / (doesn't)** have to get up early.
2 Mum **has / have / must** to go out and buy some flowers.
3 It's Uncle Bob's birthday on Friday. We **doesn't / must / mustn't** send him a card.
4 You **don't / have / mustn't** wear your glasses in the swimming pool.
5 It's Ben's party tomorrow. I **don't have / mustn't / have** forget my camera.
6 I **must / have / don't** to finish my Science project today.

Score: ..../5

C Tick (✓) the best answer.

1 These boxes are very heavy.
  a Good idea! ✗
  b I'll carry them. ✓

2 I've got a headache.
  a You should drink more water. ☐
  b You should work harder at school. ☐

3 Would you like to see my photos?
  a Yes, please. ☐
  b That's OK. ☐

4 I want to speak French.
  a You should find a French penfriend. ☐
  b You shouldn't read French books. ☐

5 Let's wash mum's car.
  a Don't worry. ☐
  b Good idea. ☐

Score: ..../4

D Choose and write.

make some sandwiches?   when you were little?   a question?
a present for our teacher?   your letter for you?   my teacher about this?
~~to eat something?~~

1 Would you like *to eat something?*
2 Could you ride a bike ....
3 Shall we buy ....
4 Should I talk to ....
5 Shall I post ....
6 Can I ask you ....

Score: ..../5

Grammar Time 3

Quiz 12

Name: .... Date: .... Total: ..../20

A Write one word.

1 ...*When*...... Beth got up, her parents were having breakfast.
2 When we saw Peter, he .... going home.
3 Aunt Liz was waiting for me .... I arrived at the station.
4 .... were you doing at lunchtime yesterday?
5 It .... raining when I got up this morning.
6 While we .... having dinner, the phone rang.

Score: ..../5

B Tick (✓) the correct sentence in each pair.

1 a Jack watched TV when I phoned. ✗
  b Jack was watching TV when I phoned. ✓
2 a While I was doing my homework, I heard a strange noise.
  b While I was doing my homework, I was hearing a strange noise.
3 a Dad was washing the car when it started to rain.
  b Dad is washing the car when it started to rain.
4 a I was looking for my keys when I have found the book.
  b I was looking for my keys when I found the book.
5 a When I came into the room, my mum and dad were dancing!
  b When I came into the room, my mum and dad was dancing!

Score: ..../4

C Choose and circle the correct question tag.

1 You haven't got any pets, **(have you?)** / **haven't you?** / **hasn't it?**
2 You can swim, **don't you?** / **can you?** / **can't you?**
3 Mum likes flowers, **does she?** / **isn't she?** / **doesn't she?**
4 You didn't phone me last night, **did you?** / **don't you?** / **didn't you?**
5 I'm your best friend, **isn't I?** / **aren't I?** / **am I?**

Score: ..../4

D Find the extra, incorrect word in each question.

1 How ~~What~~ many pupils are there in your class?
2 What are is the names of your best friends?
3 Which book is the your favourite?
4 How often do you read English capital books?
5 What time do you finish school of on Fridays?
6 Where do you your live?
7 What is the country biggest city in the world?

Score: ..../6

E Write the extra words from Exercise D. Then answer the question.

What ....? ....

Score: ..../1

Progress Check 1 (Units 1–5)

Name: .... Date: .... Total: ..../40

A Complete with *am*, *is* or *are*.

1 Harry and Beth ...*are*........ students.
2 This .... Peter.
3 How old .... you?
4 Harry and I .... neighbours.
5 Hurry up! We .... late for school.
6 Lucy .... Peter's sister.
7 I can't find Cosmo and Bella. Where .... they?
8 Here's a copy of *Grammar Time*. It .... our English book.
9 A: Are you from London?
   B: Yes, I ....

Score: ..../8

B Complete the table.

Singular	Plural
foot	1 *feet*
friend	2 ....
3	leaves
4	people
woman	5 ....

Score: ..../4

C Read, choose and write.

Sam is my brother. 1 ...*This*...... is our room.
This is my desk and 2 ....'s his desk.
These are my books and 3 .... are his books.
Look! This 4 .... my favourite photo.
It's a photo of 5 .... iguana in London Zoo.

a Those   b These   c This
a these   b that   c those
a this   b those   c that
a is   b am   c are
a an   b a   c –

Score: ..../4

D Put the apostrophe in the correct place.

1 My ...*uncle's*.... car is a Ferrari.
2 My parents car is really old.
3 The childrens toys are in the green box.
4 Here are Beth and Lucys milkshakes.
5 My brothers names are Marco and Juan.
6 My best friends name is Mandy.
7 Look at those mens clothes!

Grammar Time 3

8 The girls bikes are at the back of the house.
9 Charles hair is very short.

Score: ..../8

E Complete with *have* or *has*.

1 My sister ..*has*........ got long hair.
2 .... your school got a swimming pool?
3 We ....n't got a dog or a cat.
4 A: Have you got a bike?   B: Yes, I ....
5 Be quiet! Mum .... got a headache.

Score: ..../4

F Read, choose and write.

A: ¹ ..*Whose*..... is this umbrella?   a Whose   b Who   c Where
B: It's ² ....   a my   b me   c mine
A: Is that ³ .... bike over there? a your   b your   c you
B: No, it's ⁴ .... brother's.   a my   b yours   c you
A: Are these your glasses?
B: No, they're ⁵ ....!   a he   b her   c yours

Score: ..../4

G Complete the answers. Use prepositions of place.

1 Where are the chairs?   They're ..*opposite*.. the bed.
2 Where's Pete's laptop?   It's .... the door.
3 Where are his shoes?   They're .... the bed.
4 Where's his T-shirt?   It's .... the bed.
5 Where's his football?   It's .... the toothbrush and the cap.

Score: ..../4

H Complete with *Is there* and *Are there*. Then answer the questions about the picture in Exercise G.

1 ..*Is there*........ a TV in Pete's room?   ..*No, there isn't.*......
2 .... two guitar's in Pete's room?   ....
3 .... two desks in Pete's room?   ....
4 .... a laptop in Pete's room?   ....
5 .... a chimpanzee in Pete's room?   ....

Score: ..../4

Progress Check 2 (Units 6–10)

Name: .... Date: .... Total: ..../40

A Complete the sentences. Use *don't* or *let's*.

1. It's a lovely day. ..Let's.. go to the park.
2. I've got a headache. .... play the piano.
3. I'm thirsty. .... make a fruit cocktail.
4. I'm bored. .... play a game.
5. .... play near the road. It's dangerous.

Score: ..../4

B Complete the sentences. Use the words in the box.

~~her~~   him   it   me   them

1. She's so funny! Look at ..her..
2. Where are my glasses? I can't find ....
3. Where's Peter. I can't see ....
4. Hey! That's my sandwich. Don't eat ....
5. I'm OK. Don't worry about ....

Score: ..../4

C Read, choose and write.

1. Jon ..visits.. his aunt every week.   a doesn't   b visits   c don't
2. Peter plays basketball .... Saturdays. a in   b at   c on
3. My dog .... like cats.   a don't   b doesn't   c does
4. Do you watch TV .... the mornings? a in   b at   c on
5. The Earth .... round the sun.   a going   b go   c goes
6. Lucy plays the violin .... five o'clock. a in   b at   c on
7. My sister .... shopping.   a hates   b love   c like
8. I .... my room once a week.   a tidy   b tidies   c don't
9. It sometimes snows .... Christmas day. a in   b on   c at

Score: ..../8

D Look and write questions and answers.

	always	usually	often	sometimes	never
Cosmo and Bella			have milk		get up early
Harry			watch TV	get up late	
Beth	get up early	walk to school			

Grammar Time 3

1 Cosmo and Bella / have milk / often?
  Do Cosmo and Bella often have milk? Yes, they do.
2 Harry / get up late / always
  ....
3 Beth / walk to school / usually
  ....
4 Harry / watch TV / often
  ....
5 Beth / get up late / sometimes
  ....
6 Cosmo and Bella / get up early / always
  ....

Score: ..../8

E Complete with the present simple or present continuous.

1 I *watch* .... (watch) TV every day.
2 Peter and Lucy *are watching* .... (watch) TV at the moment.
3 We .... (not go) to the park today.
4 .... (Harry / tidy) his room every day?
5 I .... (work) in London this week.
6 .... (you / brush) your teeth every morning?
7 We always .... (have) a party on my birthday.
8 .... (the baby / sleep) at the moment?
9 Mum .... (wear) her new shoes today.
10 We .... (not have) a barbecue every week.

Score: ..../8

F Complete with the –ing form or to + infinitive.

1 Do you want *to go* .... (go) to the cinema?
2 I'm not very good at *skiing* .... (ski).
3 .... (dance) is my favourite exercise.
4 We're keen on .... (visit) museums.
5 My brother loves .... (play) computer games.
6 I don't want .... (wear) that T-shirt.
7 My sister wants .... (be) a doctor.
8 My dad isn't interested in .... (shop).
9 I'd like .... (visit) London.
10 I hate .... (go) to the dentist.

Score: ..../8

74

Progress Check 3 (Units 11–15)

Name: .... Date: .... Total: ..../40

A Tick [✓] the correct box.

	Countable	Uncountable
1 sandwich	✓	☐
2 yoghurt	☐	✓
3 biscuit	☐	☐
4 cheese	☐	☐
5 apple	☐	☐
6 water	☐	☐

Score: ..../4

B Read, choose and write.

1 There isn't ....*any*........ yoghurt in the fridge.
   a any   b no   c some
2 Are there .... apples in that bowl?
   a any   b no   c some
3 Listen! There's .... downstairs.
   a anyone   b someone   c somewhere
4 I can't find my glasses ....
   a somewhere   b anyone   c anywhere
5 There's .... milk in the fridge.
   a any   b some   c a
6 Can .... do this homework?
   a anywhere   b anything   c anyone
7 There are .... children in the park.
   a any   b a   c some
8 There are .... apples on the table.
   a any   b no   c anyone
9 There aren't .... bananas in the bowl.
   a no   b some   c any

Score: ..../8

Photocopiable © Pearson Education Limited 2008

Grammar Time 3

C Write *much*, *many* or *a lot of*.

1 How ..*many*.. hot dogs have you got?
2 Are there .... shops in your town?
3 There are .... apples in that bag.
4 There isn't .... milk in Cosmo's bowl.
5 How .... students are there in your class?
6 We haven't got .... money.
7 How .... bread do we need?
8 There aren't .... tourists here today.
9 We need .... cola.

Score: ..../8

D Choose the correct word.

1 a tin of	a water	b soup	c bread
2 a slice of	a flour	b pizza	c chocolate
3 a bottle of	a water	b bread	c flour
4 a loaf of	a pizza	b soup	c bread
5 a carton of	a milk	b chocolate	c flour

Score: ..../4

E Write *was* or *were*.

1 ..*Were*.. you at home yesterday afternoon?
2 There ....n't many pupils at my mum's school.
3 I .... very busy yesterday.
4 .... Mark at the supermarket with you?
5 We .... at the cinema yesterday afternoon.
6 My friends .... all at the sports centre last weekend.
7 There ....n't any supermarkets a hundred years ago.
8 The party was terrible! There .... n't any music.
9 Where .... you last night?

Score: ..../8

F Complete with the past simple.

1 Peter and Harry ..*saw*.. (see) Ben Baker at the supermarket.
2 I .... (finish) my homework an hour ago.
3 My dad .... (buy) some flowers for my mum.
4 Our teacher .... (have) a headache this morning.
5 We .... (visit) a lot of museums in London.
6 Maria .... (write) a letter to her friend in France.
7 My sister and I .... (go) to the park yesterday.
8 My brother .... (find) some money in the street.
9 I .... (play) basketball last Saturday.

Score: ..../8

Progress Check 4 (Units 16–20)

Name: .... Date: .... Total: ..../40

A Read, choose and write.

1 Tigers are ...*more*...... dangerous than cats. a more b big c more
2 What is the .... animal in the cat family? a big b bigger c biggest
3 A car is .... expensive than a bicycle. a more b fast c most
4 Horses are more .... than dogs. a stronger b beautiful c faster
5 My brother is taller .... my dad. a than b more c most
6 I am the .... singer in the class. a worst b bad c worse
7 New York is the .... exciting city in the world. a than b most c more
8 My friend Sam is .... than me. a old b older c oldest
9 Who is the .... pupil in your class? a oldest b better c taller

Score: ..../8

B Complete with adverbs.

1 Peter is a good swimmer. He swims ...*well*.......
2 My uncle is a bad driver. He drives ....
3 I am a fast worker. I work ....
4 Beth is a hard worker. She works ....
5 My sister is a quick writer. She writes ....

Score: ..../4

C Choose and complete.

1 (careful, carefully)
   a This is very important. Read it ...*carefully*.....
   b You can use my camera, but be very ...*careful*..... with it.
2 (polite, politely)
   a My cousin isn't very ....
   b Ask .... and you can use my laptop.
3 (beautiful, beautifully)
   a That's a .... photograph.
   b Your sister sings ....
4 (noisy, noisily)
   a That game is really .... Please play quietly.
   b Some people eat very .... It's awful!
5 (easy, easily)
   a This game is so .... My little sister can play it.
   b I'm unhappy. I don't make friends ....

Score: ..../4

Grammar Time 3

D Complete with one word.

1 **A:** Are you ¹ *going* to go out today?
   B: Yes, I ² .... I'm going to meet my friends and we ³ .... going to ⁴ .... football. Do you want to come?
   A: No, thanks. I think ⁵ ....'s going to rain.
2 **A:** What ⁶ .... you going to do this weekend?
   B: I'm going to ⁷ .... shopping.
   A: ⁸ .... you going to buy some CDs?
   B: No, I'm ⁹ .... I've got hundreds of CDs.

Score: ..../8

E Use the words in brackets to write correct sentences.

1 I hope our team win. (will) *I hope our team will win.*
2 There will lots of people at the beach today. (be)
   There will be lots of people at the beach today.
3 I think stay in this evening. (I'll) ....
4 Will be cities on Mars in fifty years' time? (there) ....
5 Will you me tidy my room? (help) ....
6 Our town will be in twenty years' time. (different) ....
7 Will be a famous artist? (Lucy) ....
8 It will be at Aunt Agatha's. (boring) ....
9 There be many people at the party. (won't) ....
10 Mum won't us stay up late this evening. (let) ....

Score: ..../8

F Write *a/an*, *the* or –.

TeenLink

Hi! My name's Richard. I'm thirteen years old and I come from
¹ – Manchester in ² .... UK.
I like ³ .... sport very much. I play football every day. My favourite subject at ⁴ .... school is Science.
My dad is ⁵ .... teacher and my mum works in ⁶ .... office in
⁷ .... centre of Manchester.
This is ⁸ .... old photo of me. I'll give you ⁹ .... better photo soon.

Score: ..../8

Progress Check 5 (Units 21–25)

Name: .... Date: .... Total: ..../40

A Complete with the present perfect.

Are we ready for the party?
1 We ...'ve cleaned... (clean) the living room.
2 Mum .... (make) some sandwiches.
3 Dad .... (buy) some cola.
4 We .... (borrow) a lot of CDs.
5 I .... (phone) all my friends.
6 Oh no! The dogs .... (eat) the sandwiches.
7 My brother .... (break) a glass.

Score: ..../6

B Read, choose and write.

1 **A:** Have you told Sam about the party ....yet....?
   a not   b never   c yet
2 **B:** Yes, I've .... told her.
   a already   b not   c have
3 I've .... read a very good book.
   a has   b have   c just
4 I've .... heard of the Scoop Sisters.
   a never   b ever   c haven't
5 Harry .... never slept in a tent.
   a hasn't   b have   c has
6 **A:** Have you .... been on a roller coaster?
   a yet   b ever   c always
7 **B:** No, I ....
   a haven't   b have   c hasn't

Score: ..../6

C Read, choose and complete.

| Can   Could   couldn't   has to   have to   must   mustn't |

1 Tony ...has to..... finish his History project.
2 The dog has got wet feet. He .... stay in the kitchen.
3 **A:** .... I borrow your camera?
   B: No, you can't.
4 I .... sleep last night. It was very hot.
5 .... you play chess when you were little?
6 My dad loves the weekend. He doesn't .... get up early.
7 You .... eat or drink in the classroom.

Score: ..../6

Photocopiable © Pearson Education Limited 2008

Grammar Time 3

D Write *should* or *shouldn't*.

1 A: I'm tired.
B: You *shouldn't* stay up late.
2 You .... eat fruit. It's good for you.
3 A: My dog is sick.
B: You .... take him to the vet.
4 A: I've got a headache.
B: You .... play on the computer so much.
5 A: I want to lose weight.
B: You .... do some sport.

Score: ..../4

E Complete the suggestions with *Let's*, *Shall we* or *Would you like*.

1 *Shall we* get the bus?
2 .... play a game.
3 .... to borrow this DVD?
4 .... to come to my party?
5 I'm hungry. .... have lunch now?
6 .... to see the photos from my holiday?
7 .... tidy the kitchen.

Score: ..../6

F Complete with the past simple or past continuous.

Lucy **1** *was reading* (read) a book when she **2** *heard* .... (hear) a strange noise.
It **3** .... (snow) when I **4** .... (get up) this morning.
I **5** .... (see) an accident while I **6** .... (wait) for the bus.
When I **7** .... (walk) into the living room, Mum and Dad **8** .... (dance)!

Score: ..../6

G Read, choose and write.

1 Anna can speak English, *can't* .... she?
 a can't   b does   c can
2 A: .... are you laughing?
 B: Because this book is funny.
 a Why   b When   c Where
3 .... you swim when you were five?
 a Can   b Could   c Do
4 .... you see the film on TV last night?
 a Do   b Did   c Have
5 Your birthday's in January, ... it?
 a isn't   b wasn't   c doesn't
6 I'm right, ... I?
 a isn't   b wasn't   c aren't
7 A: .... car is your mum's?
 B: The white one.
 a What   b Where   c Which

Score: ..../6